This Book Belongs To

____

____

____

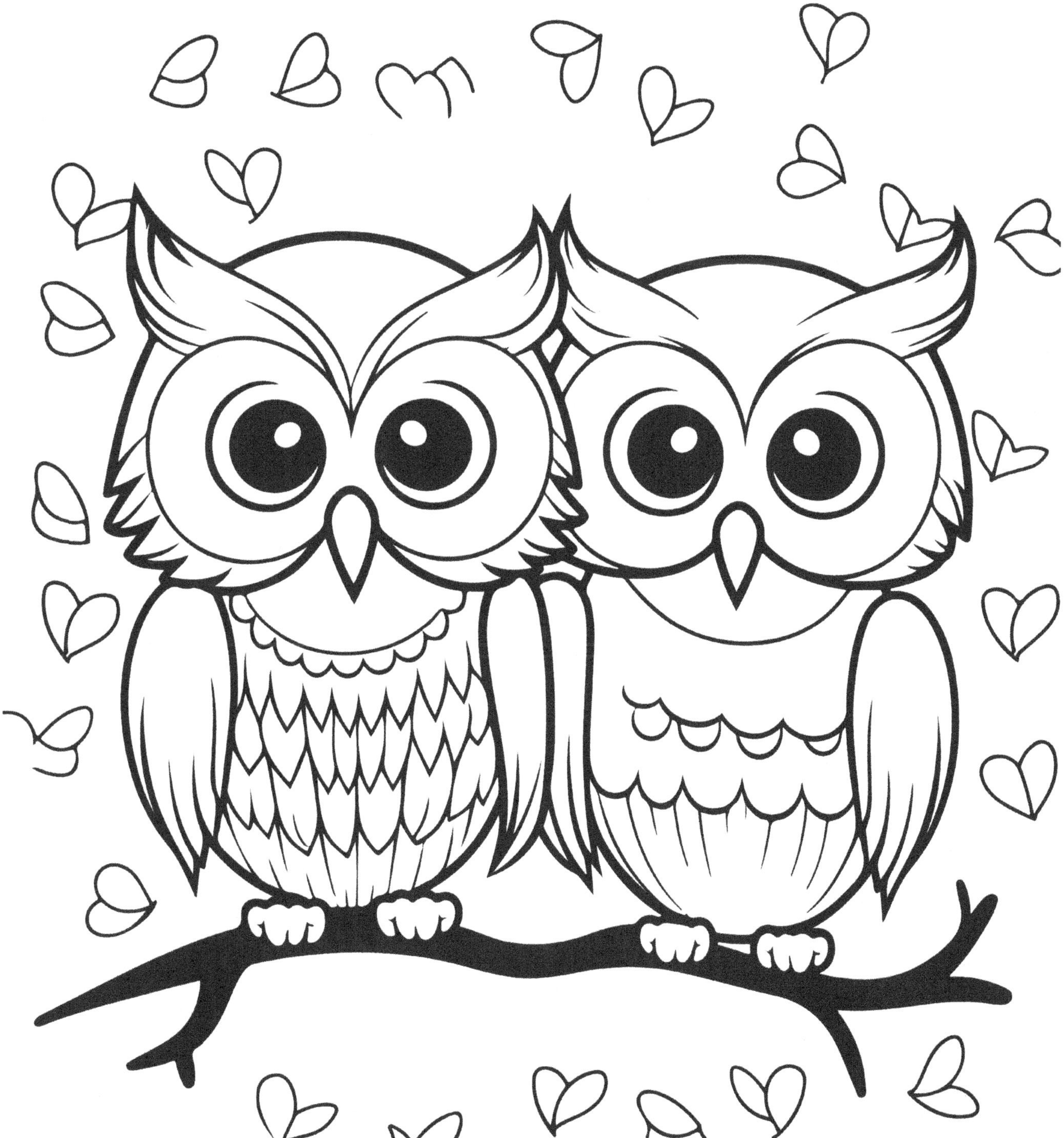

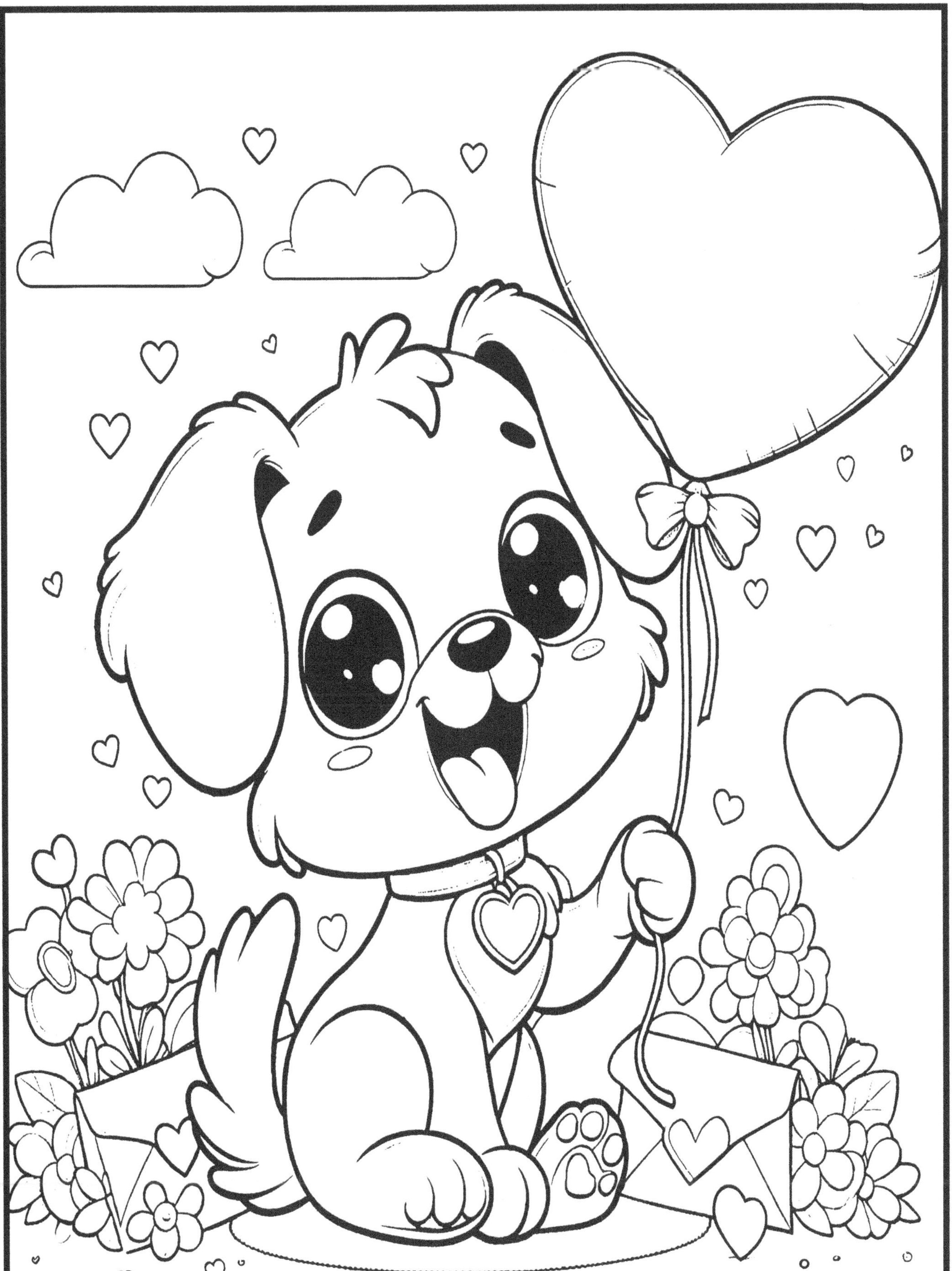

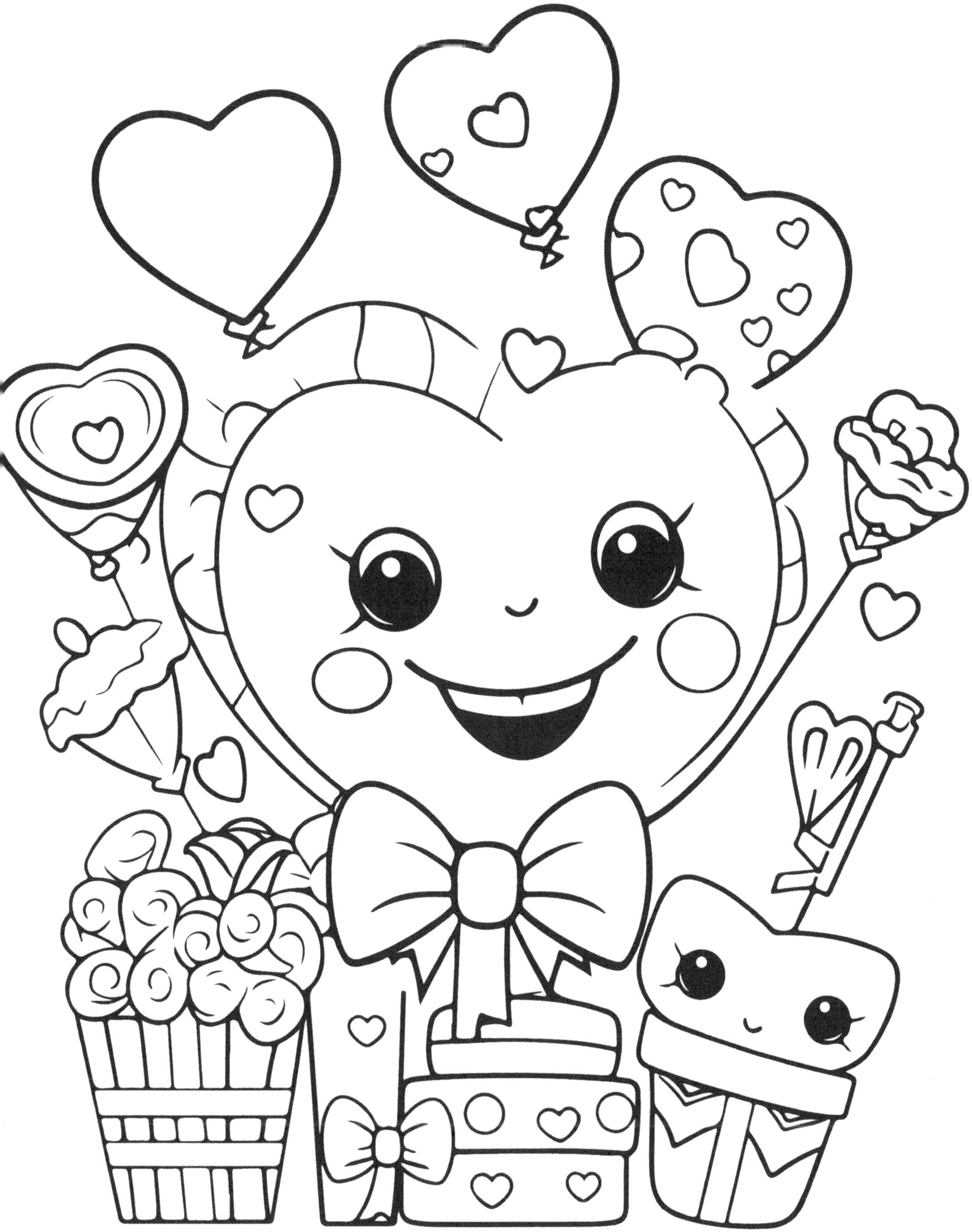

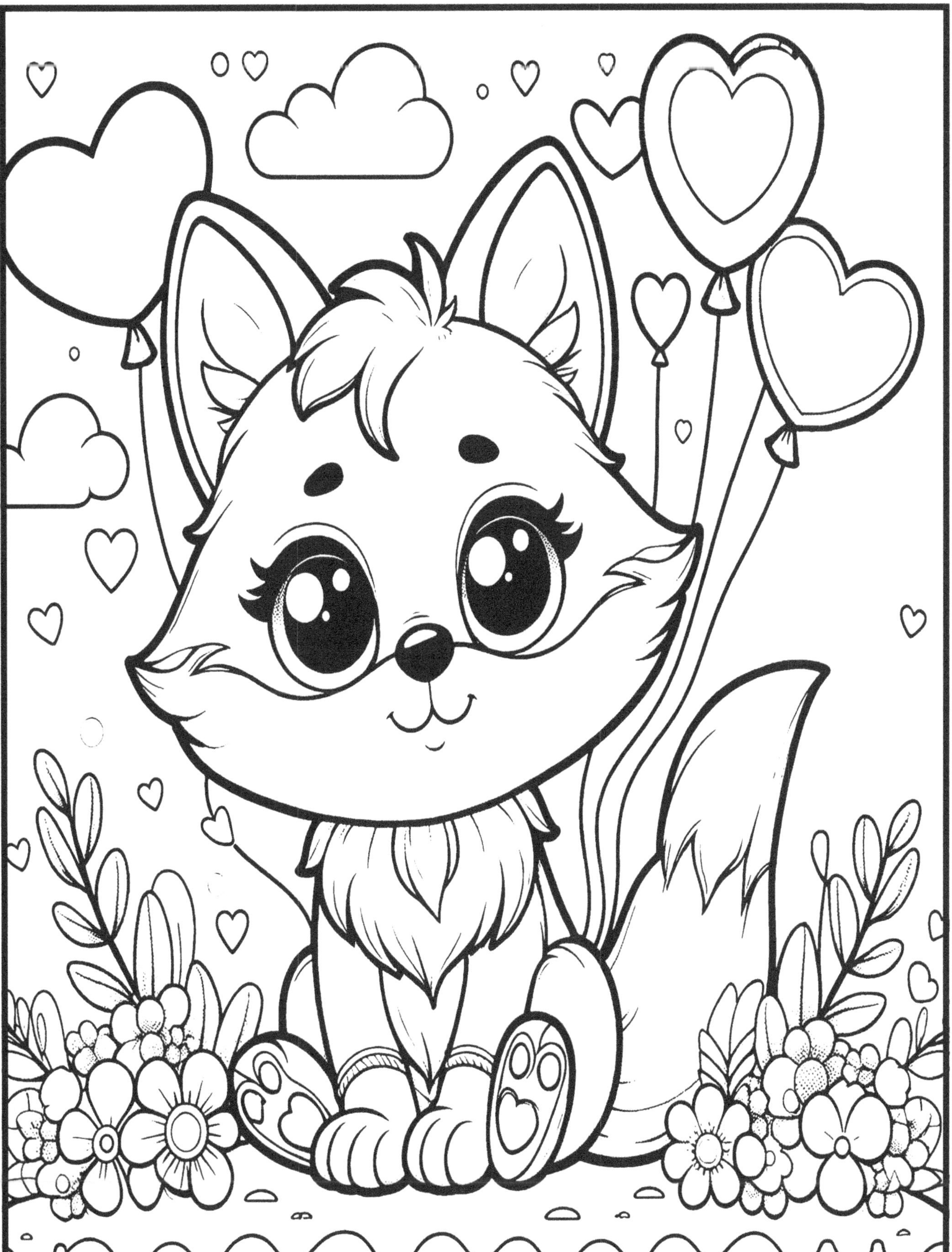

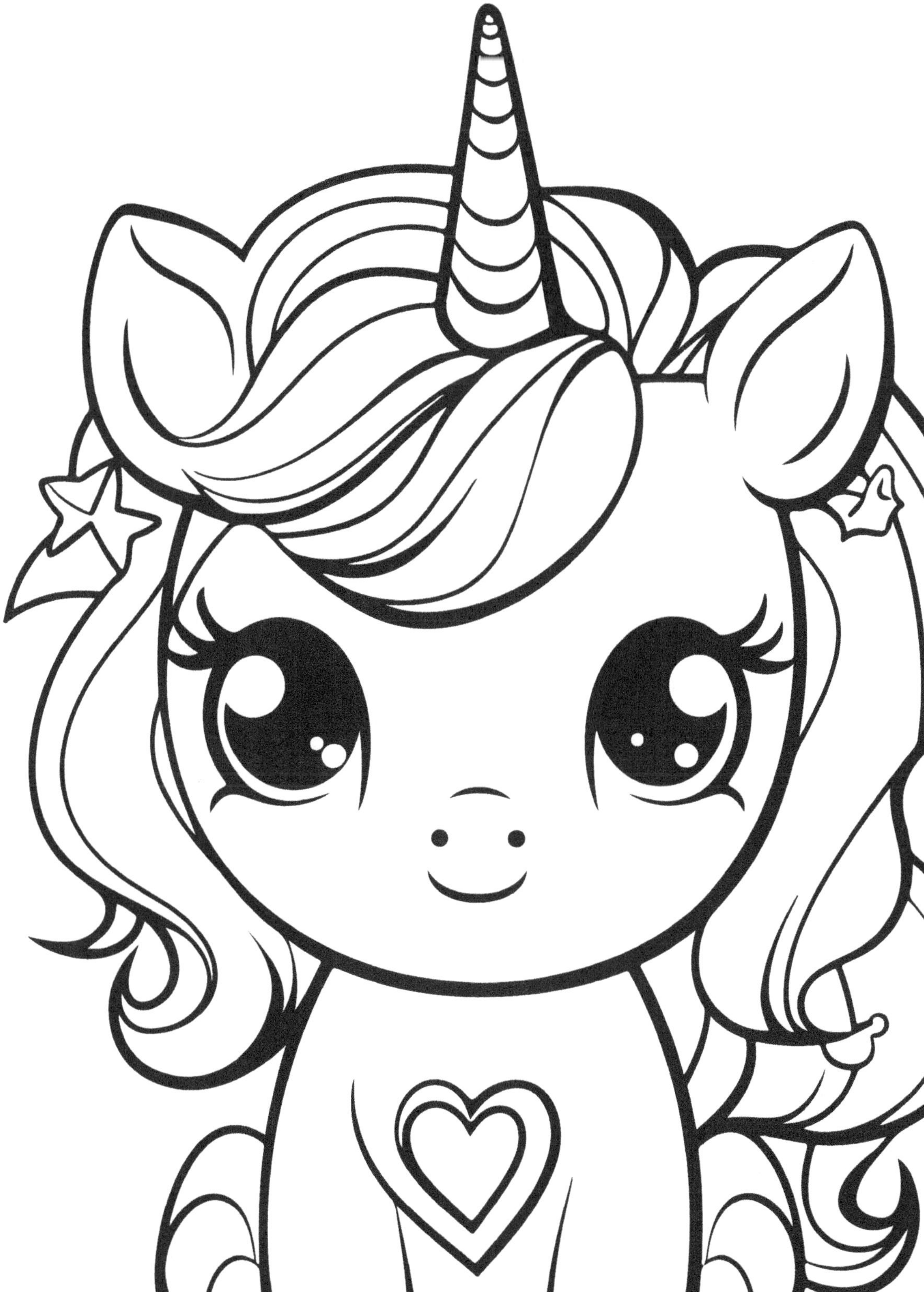

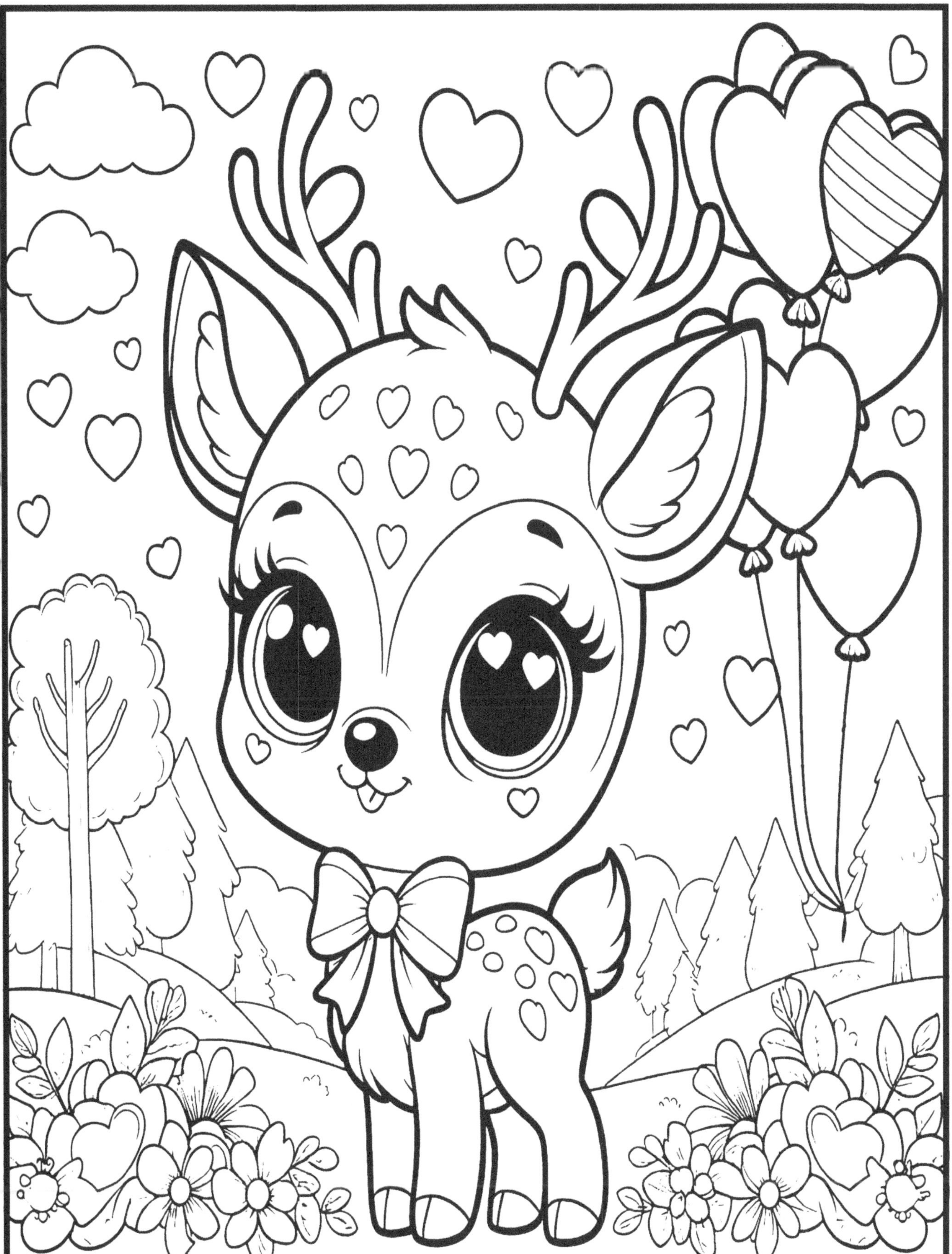

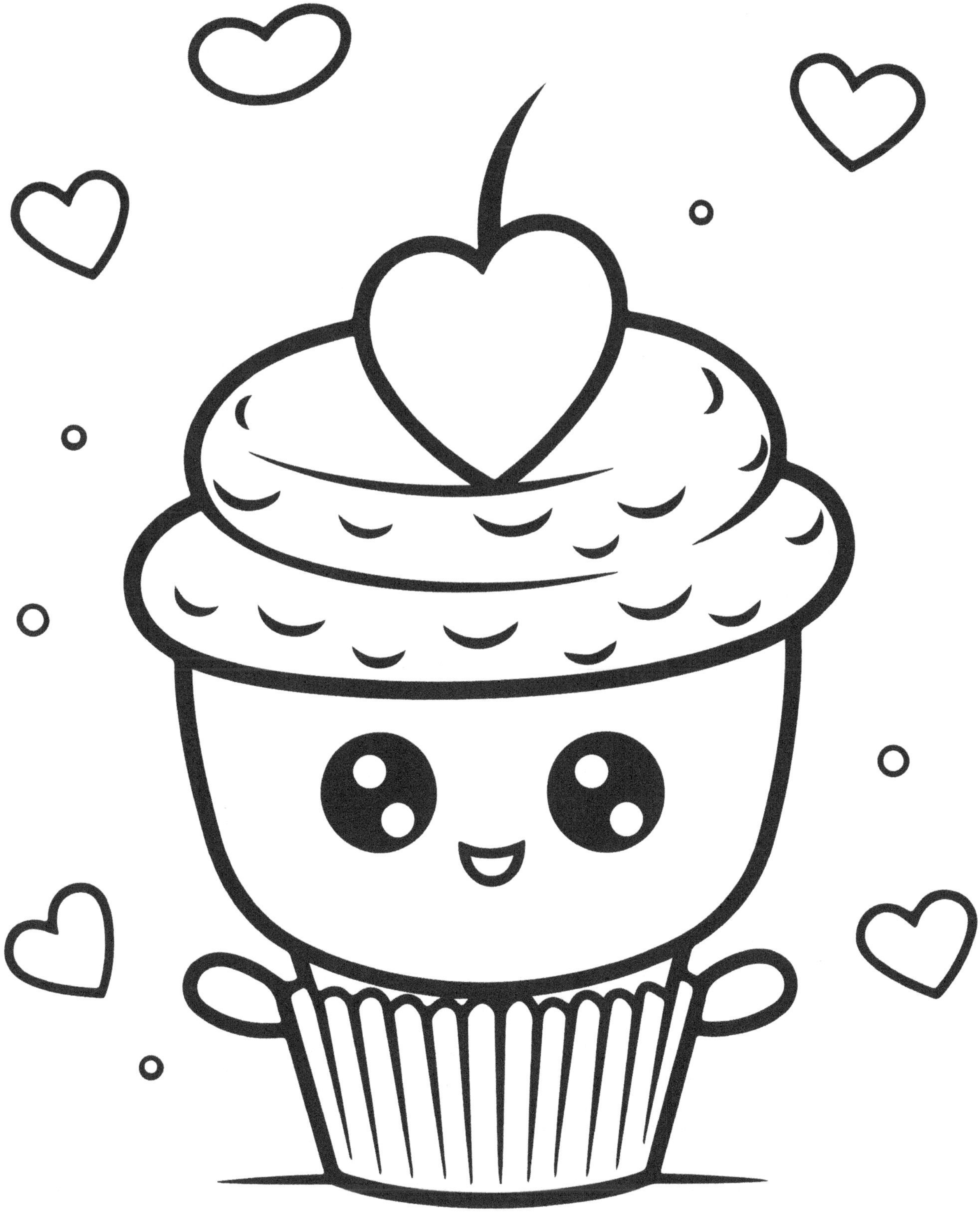

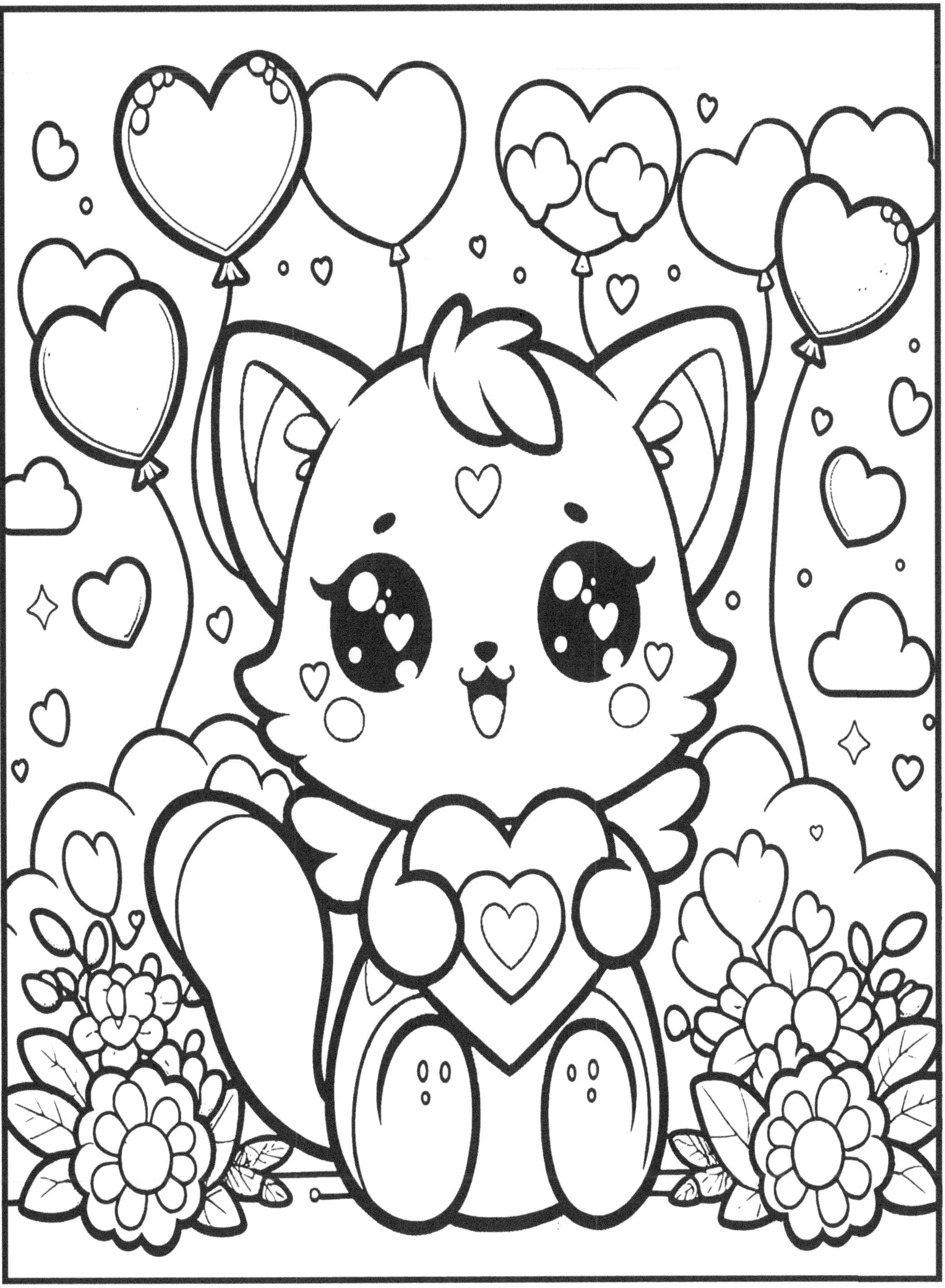

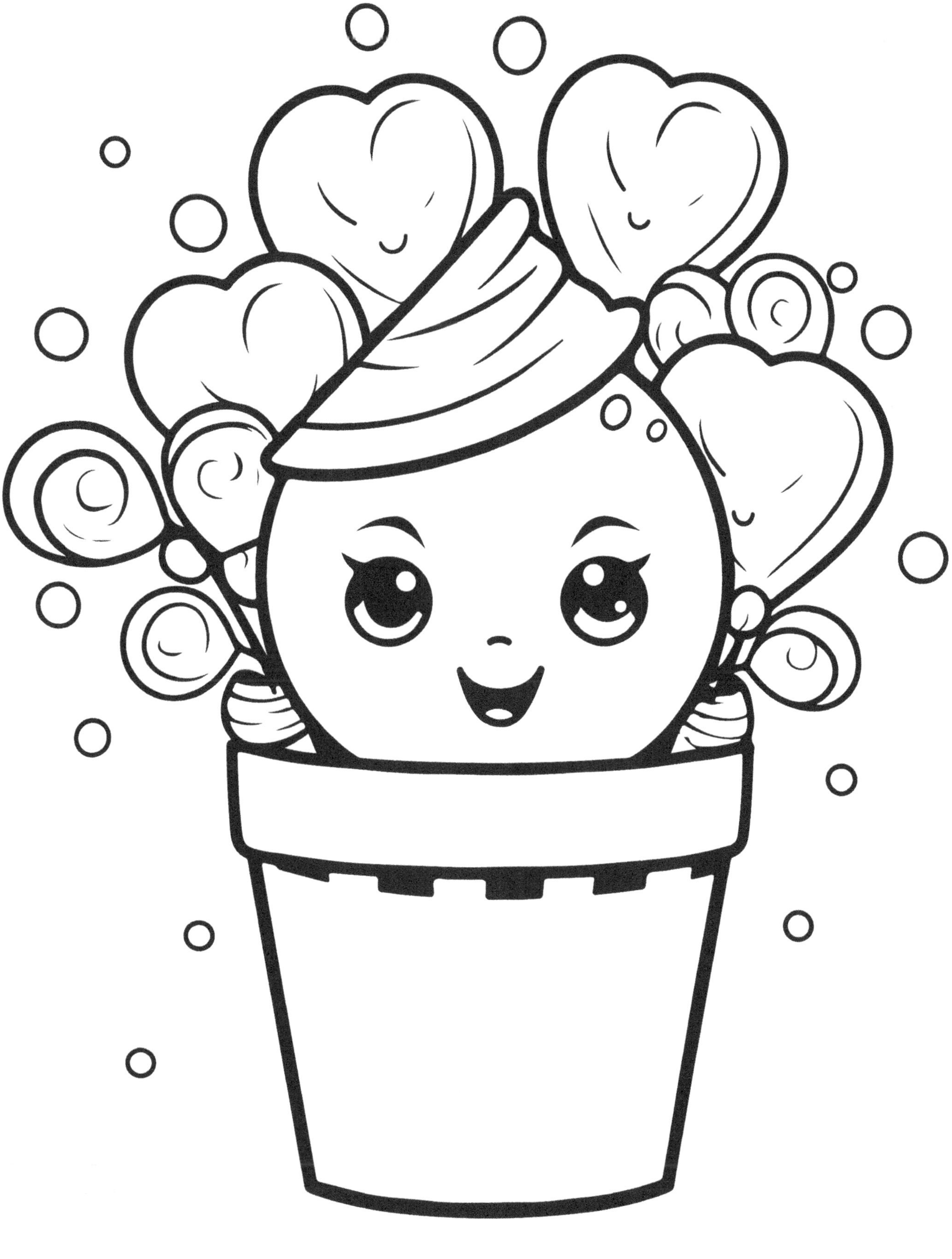

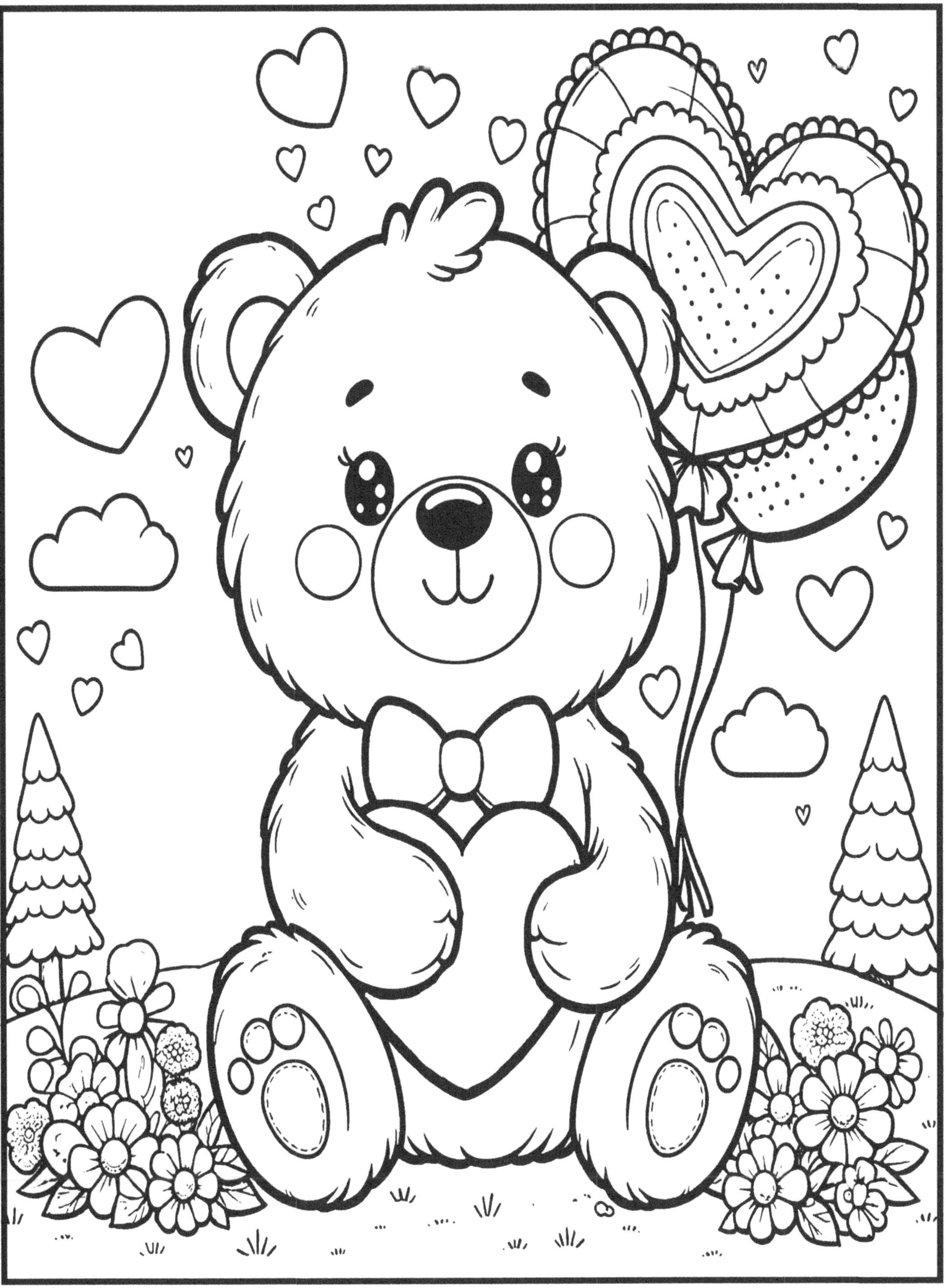

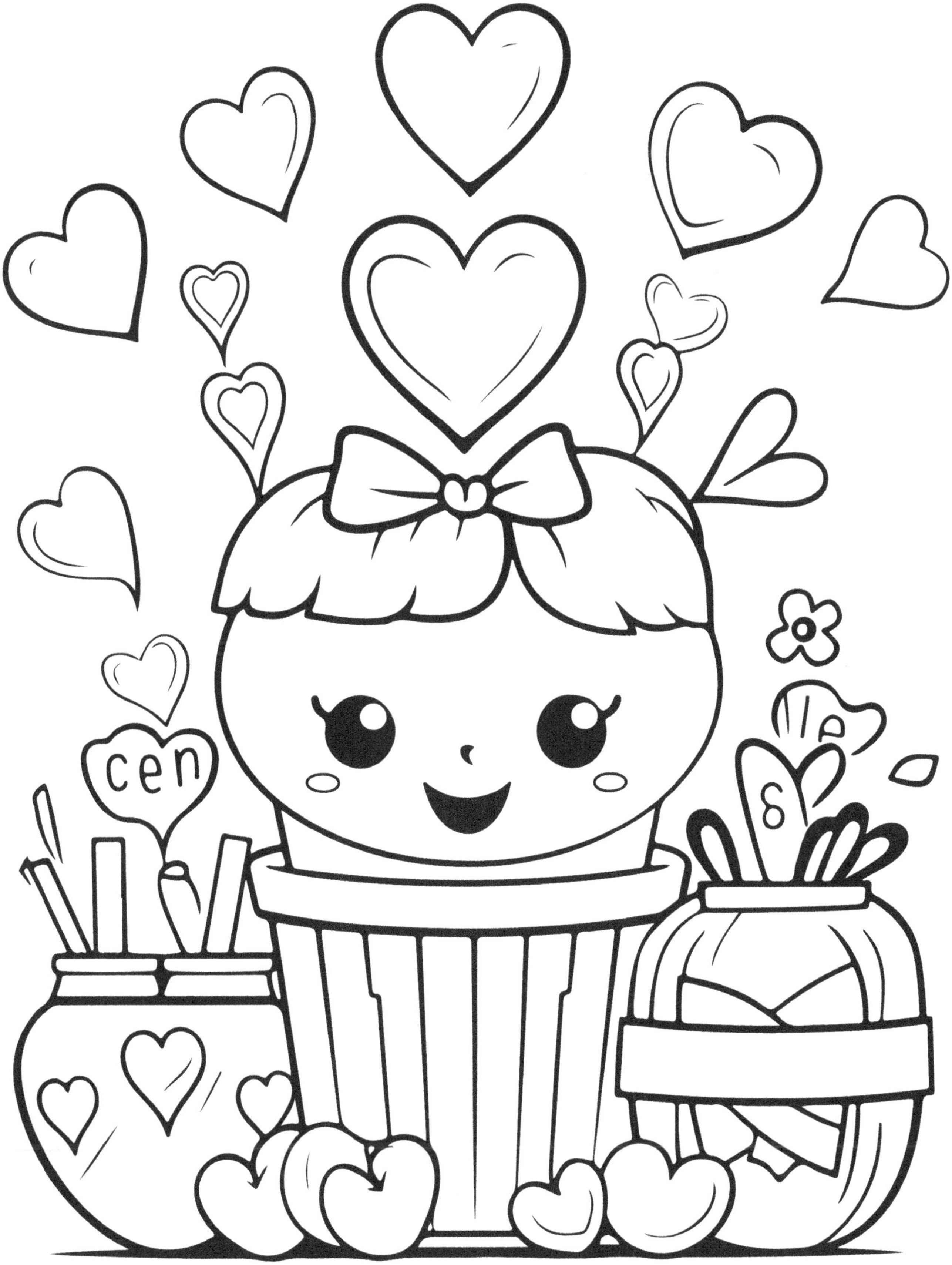
cen

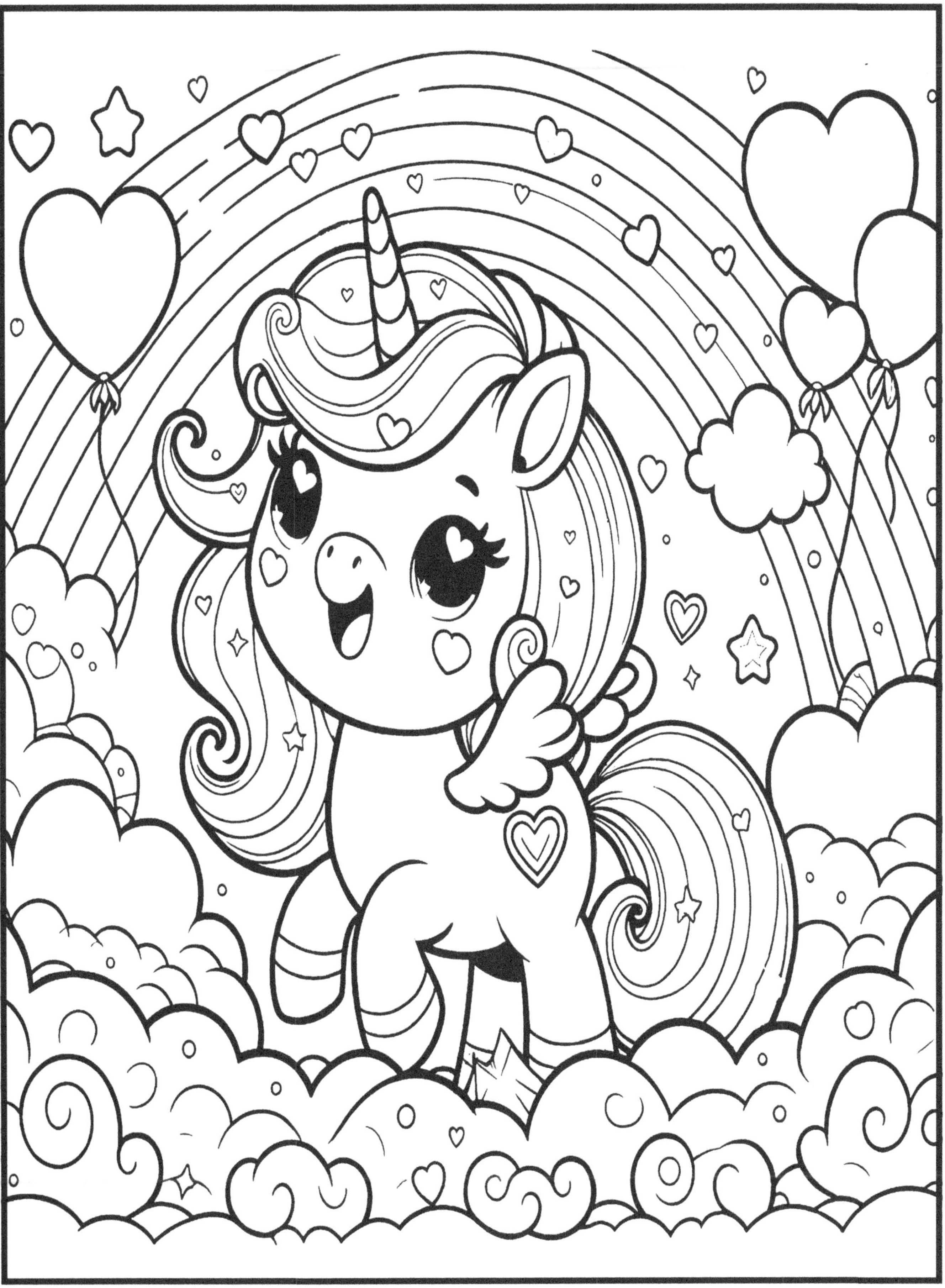

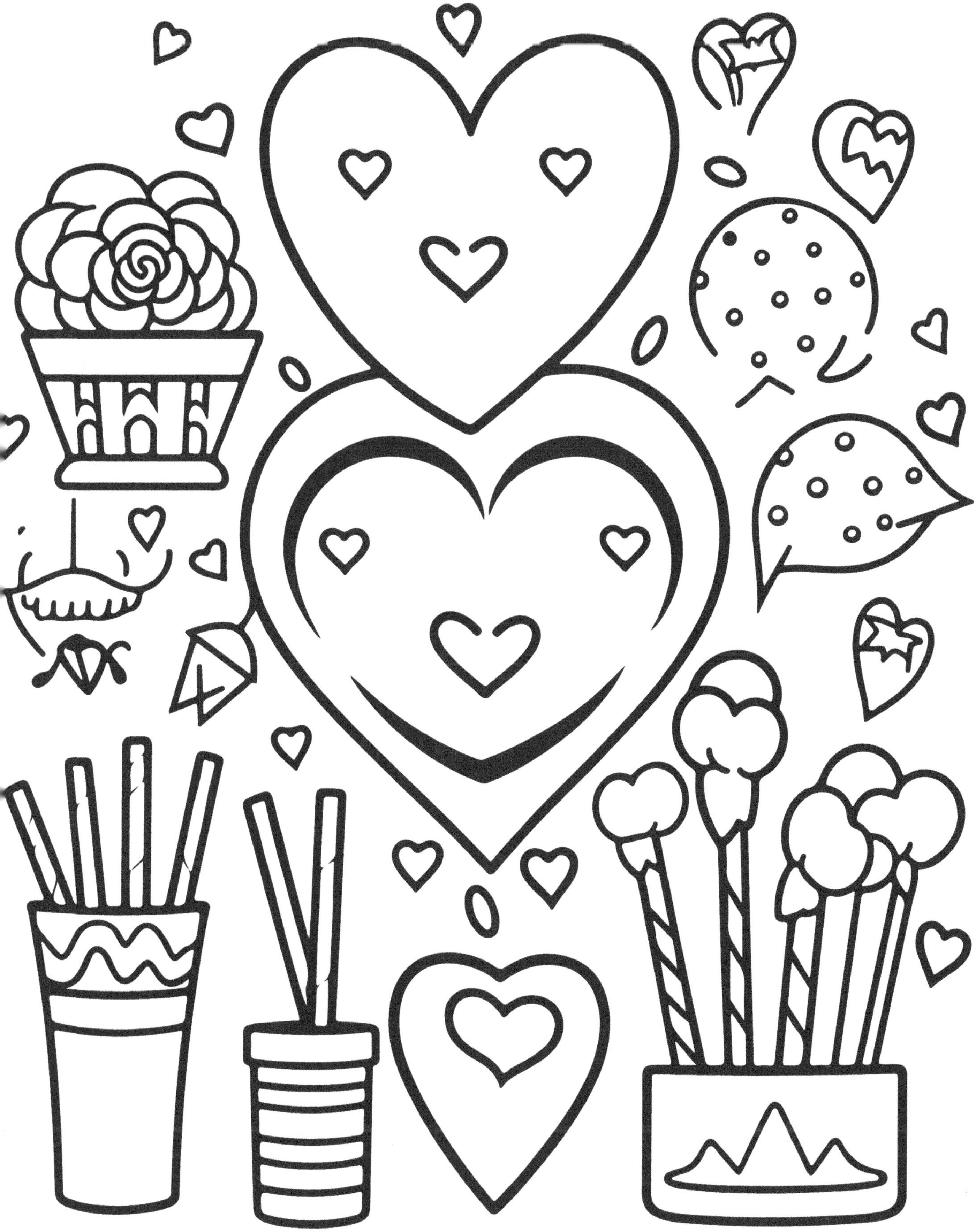

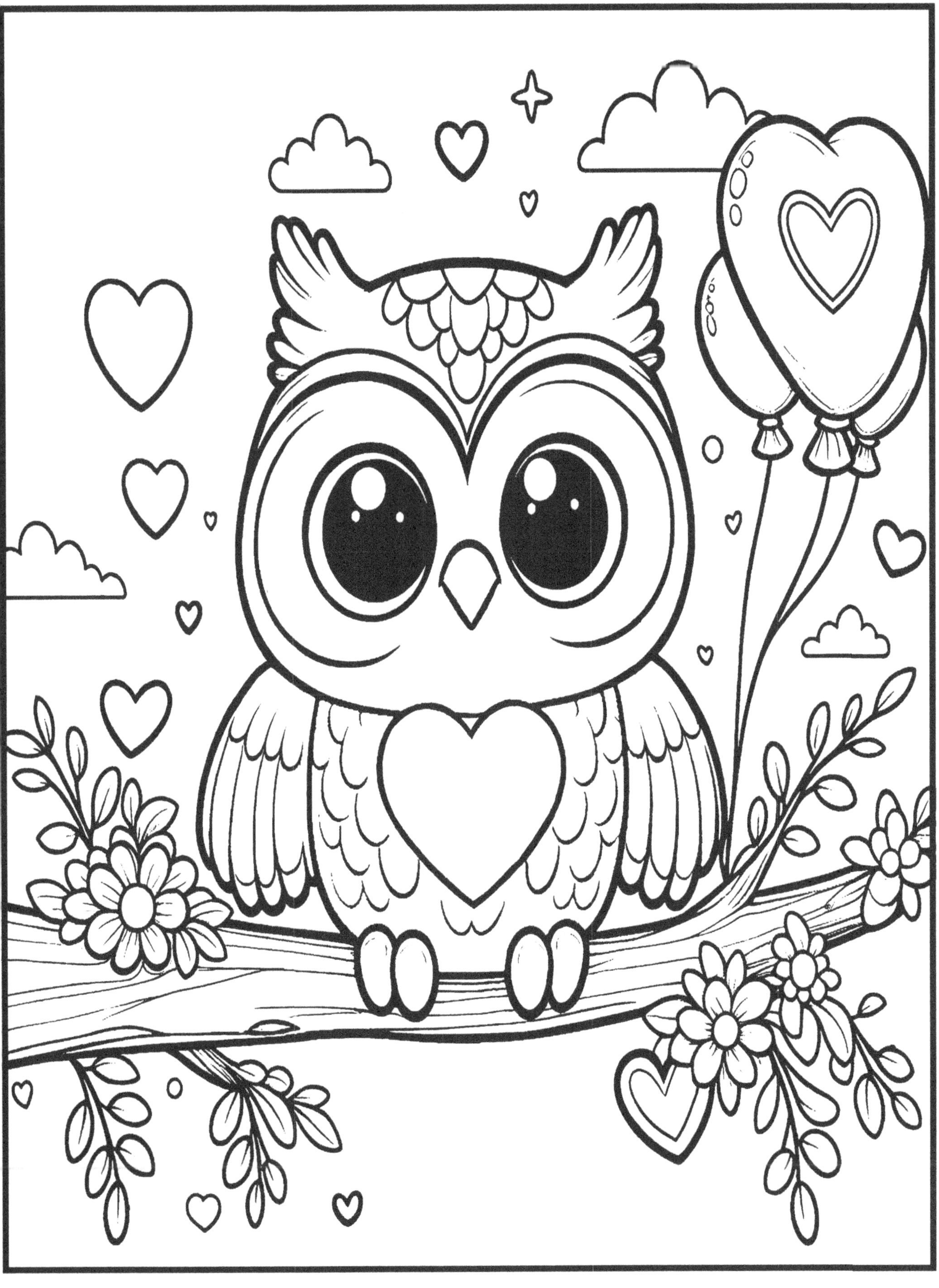

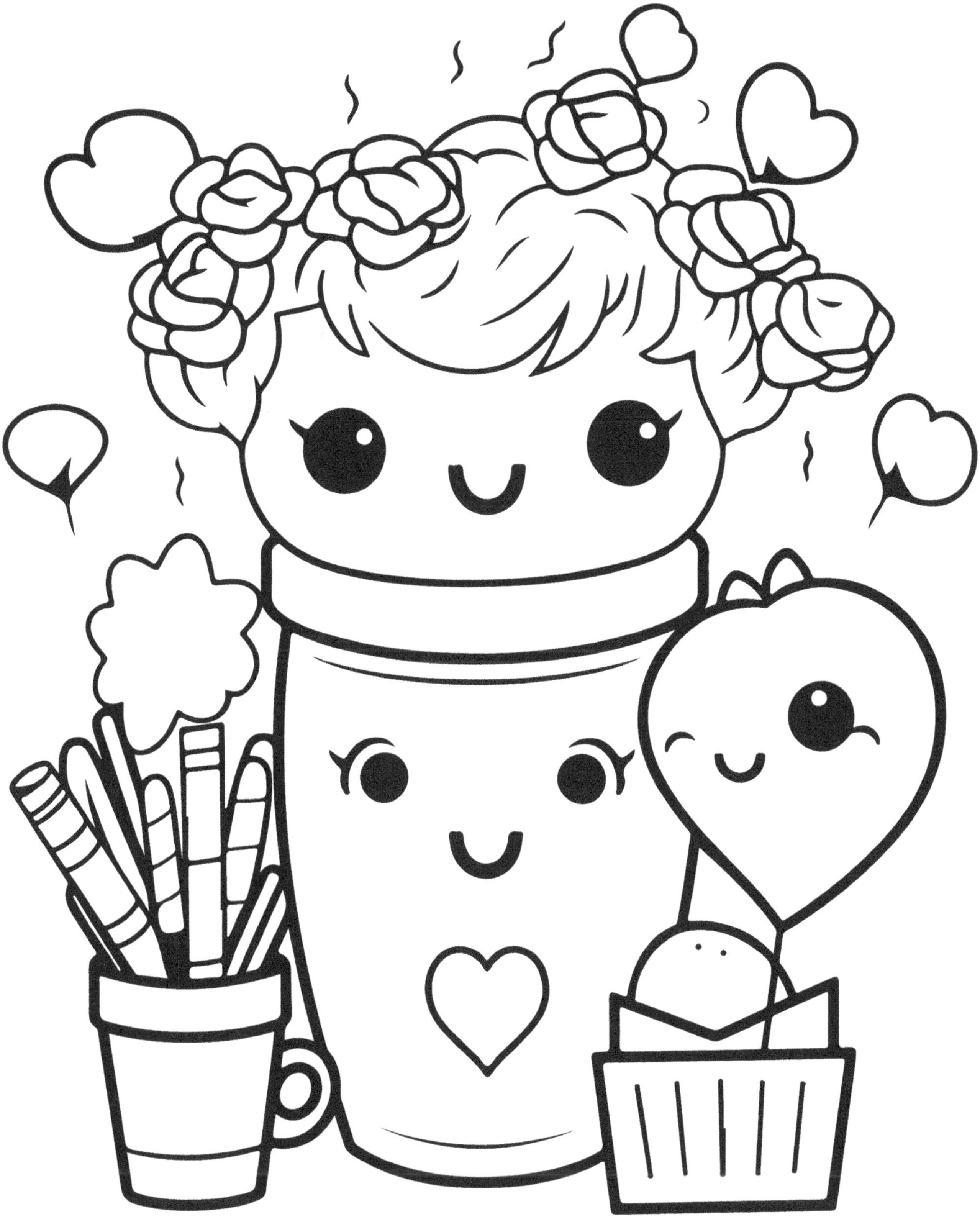

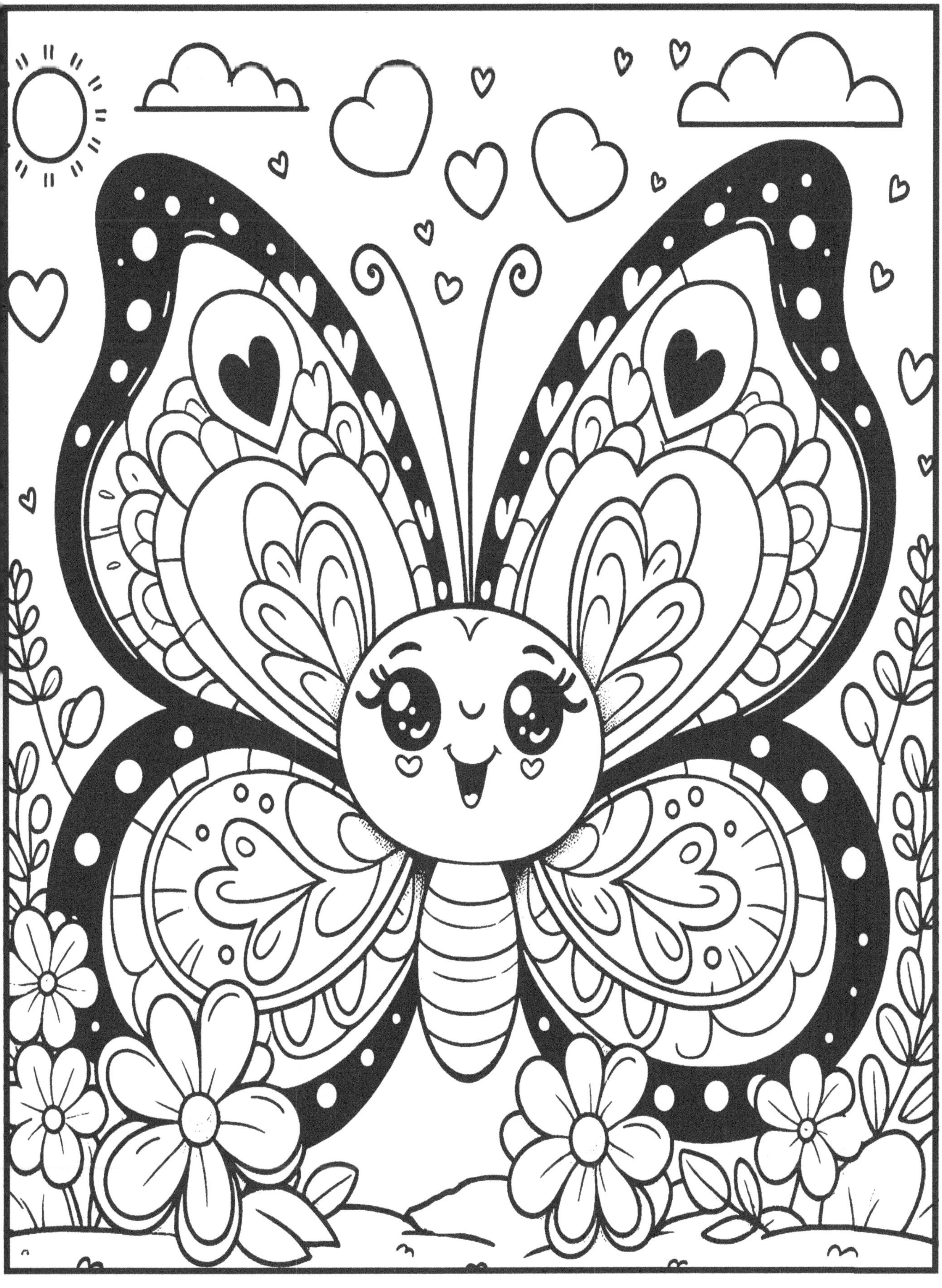

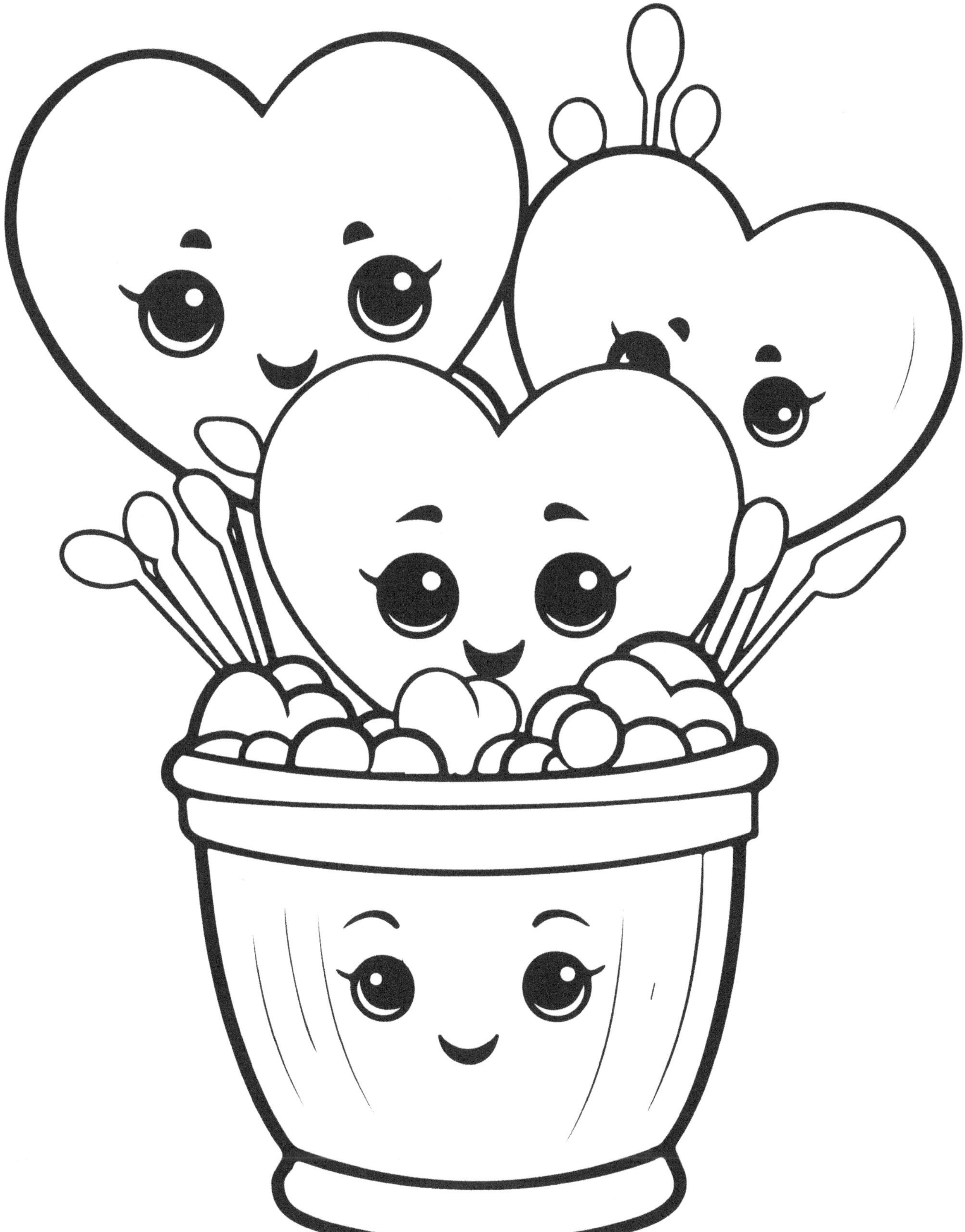

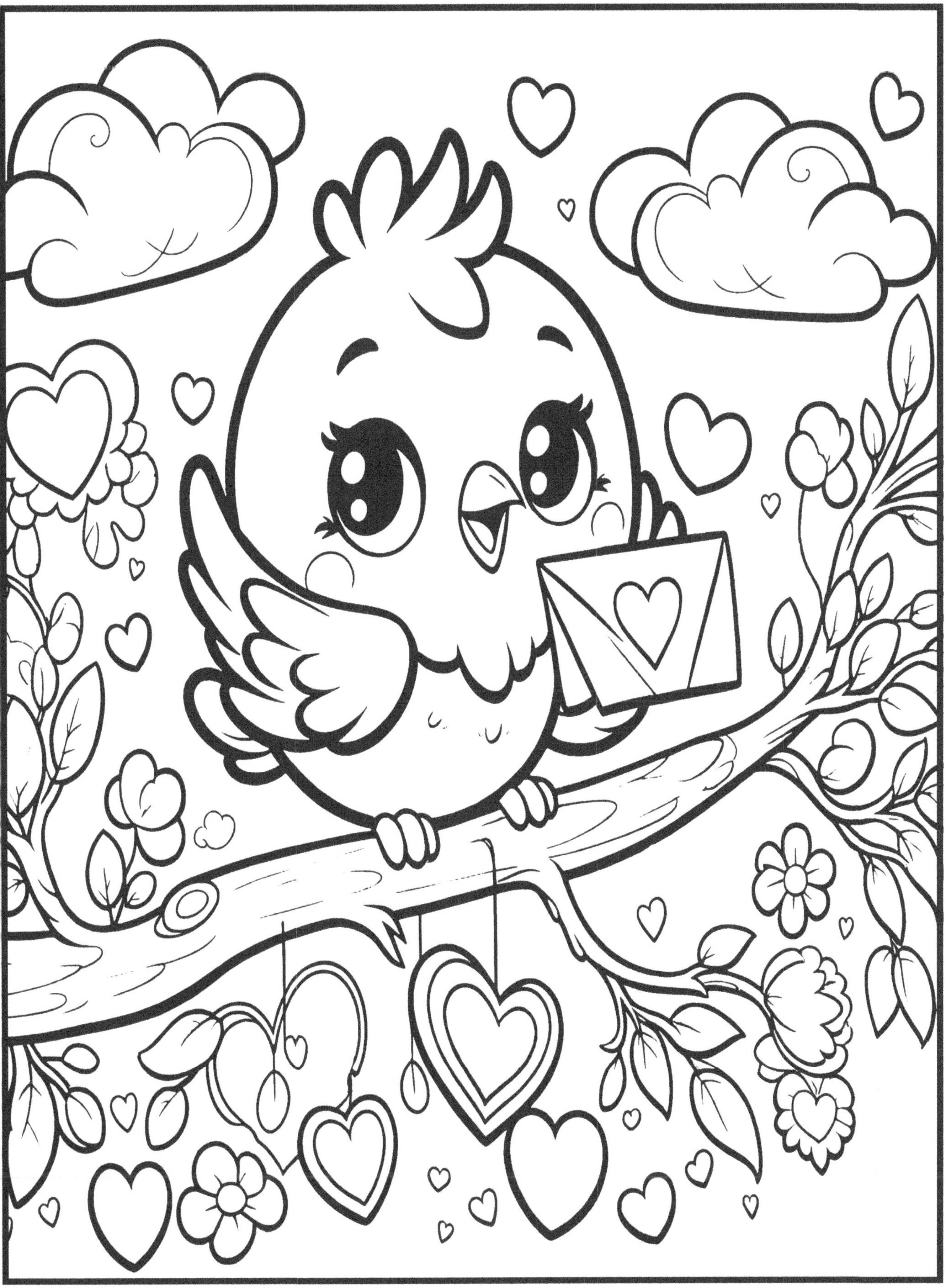

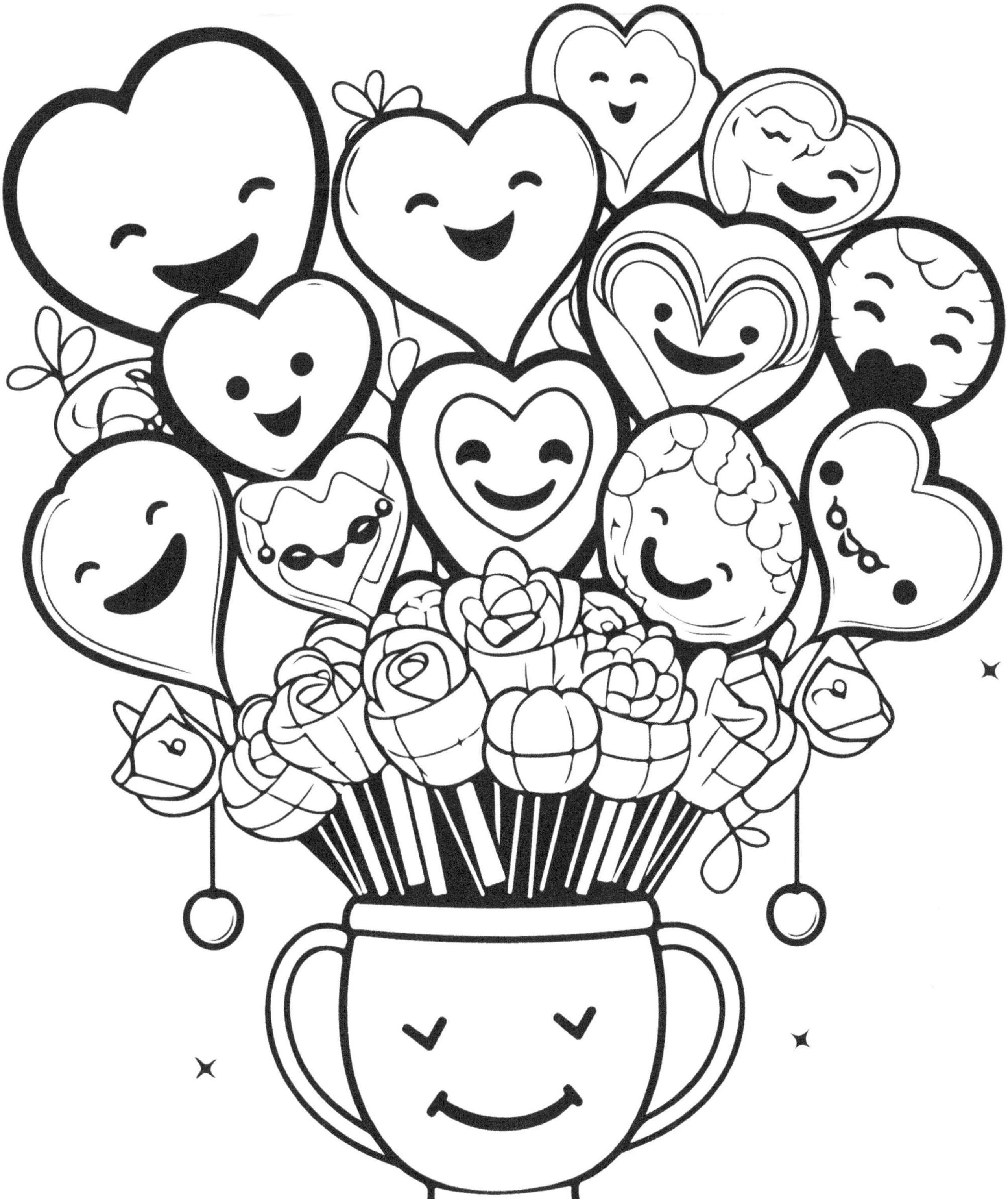

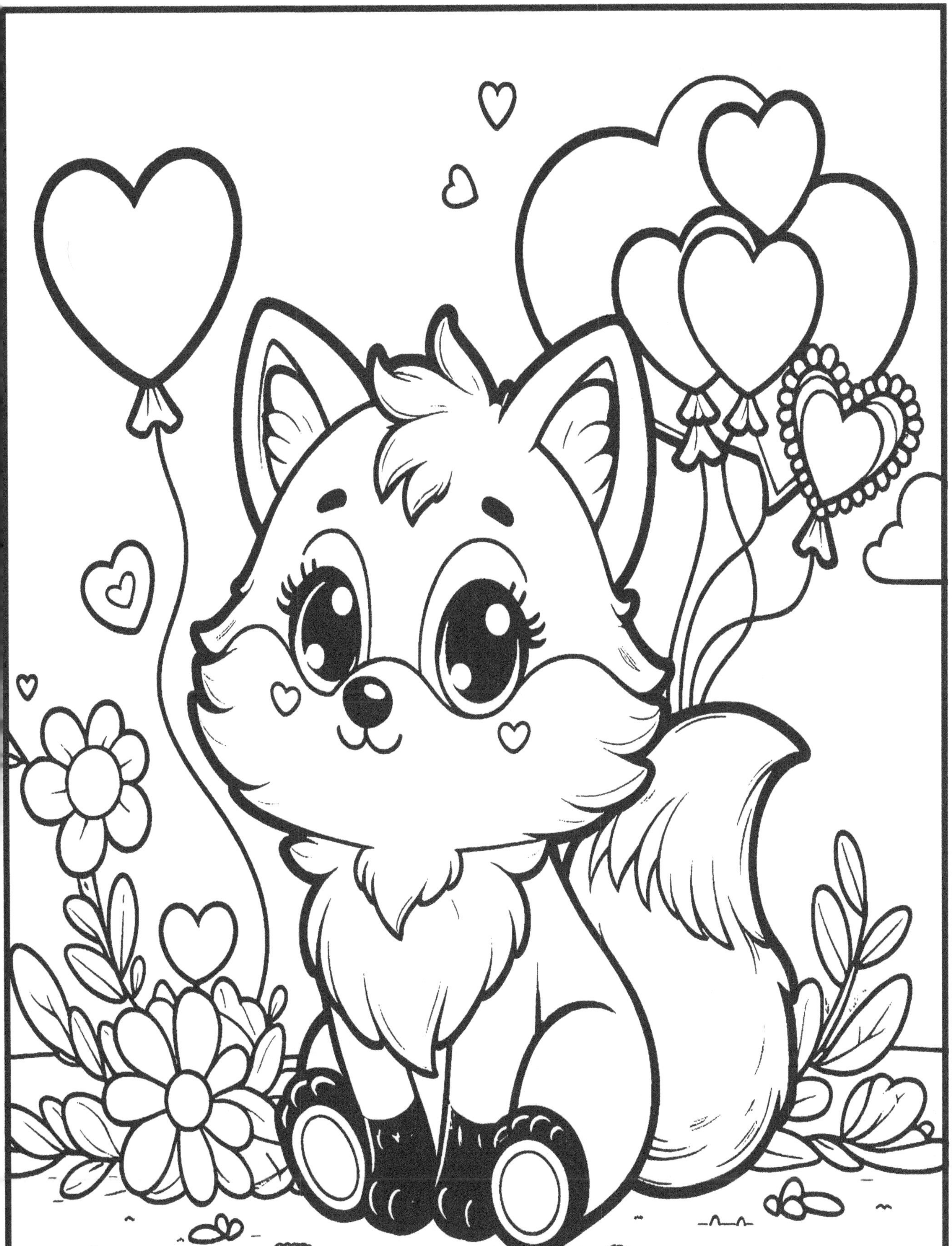

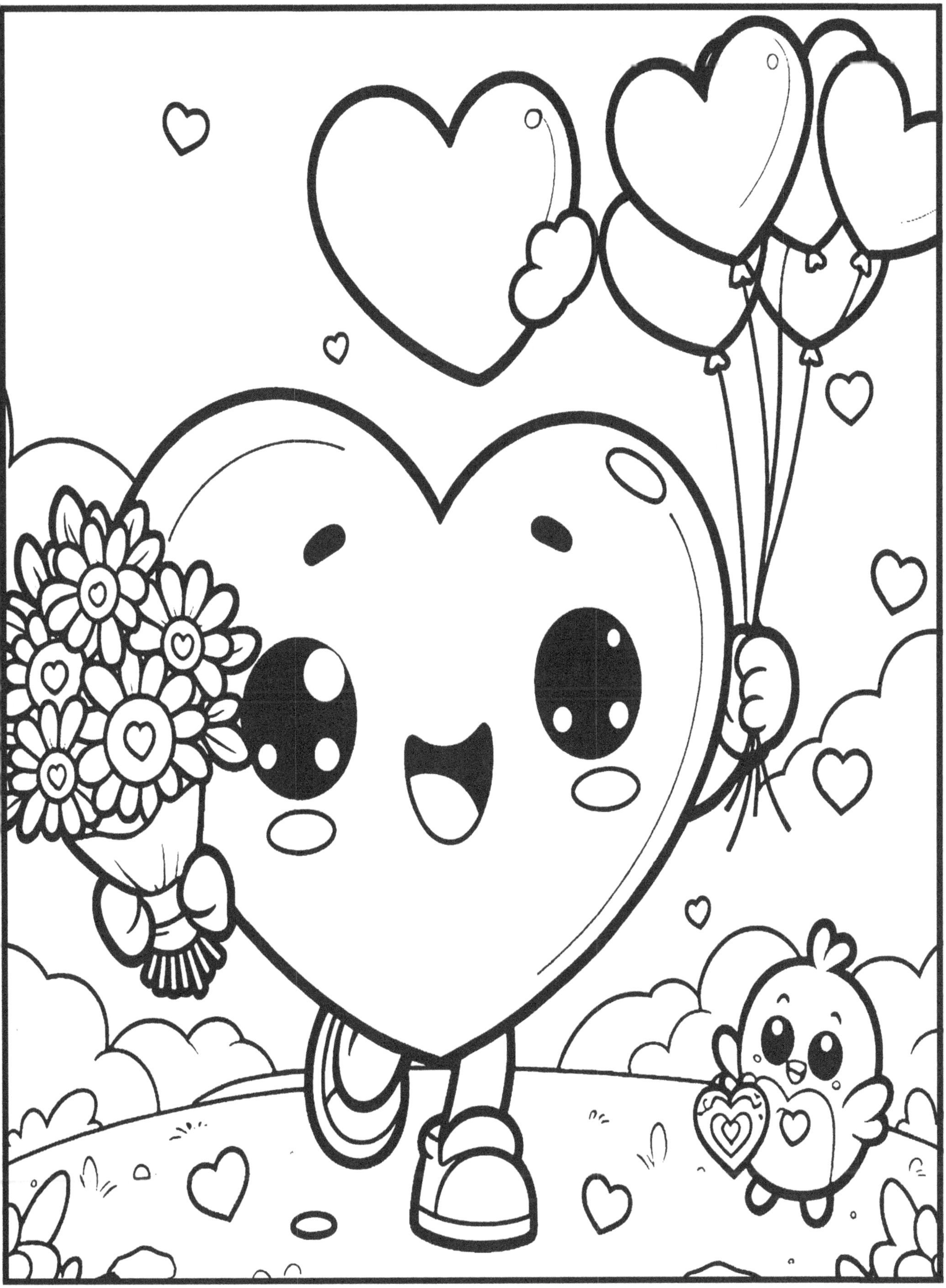

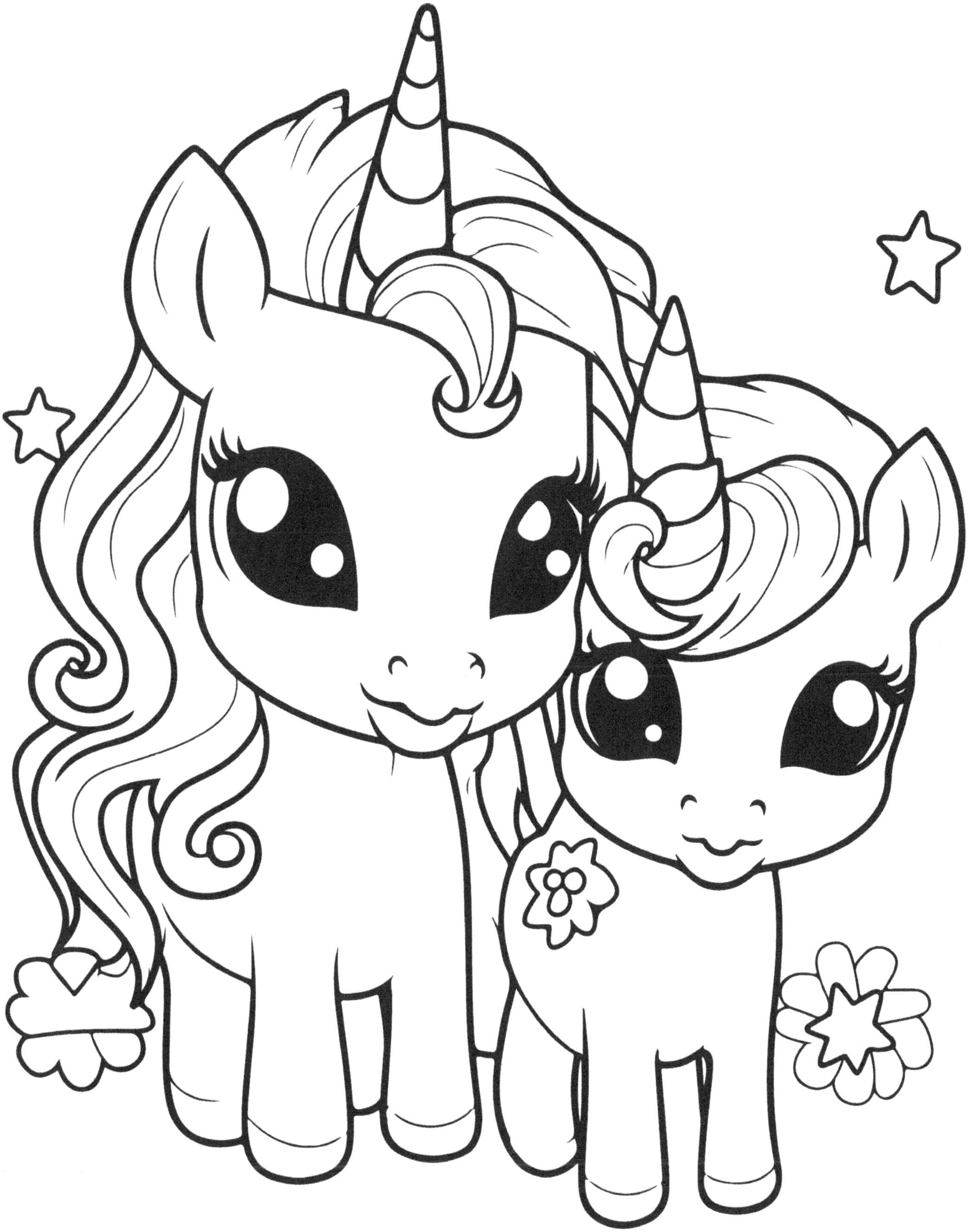

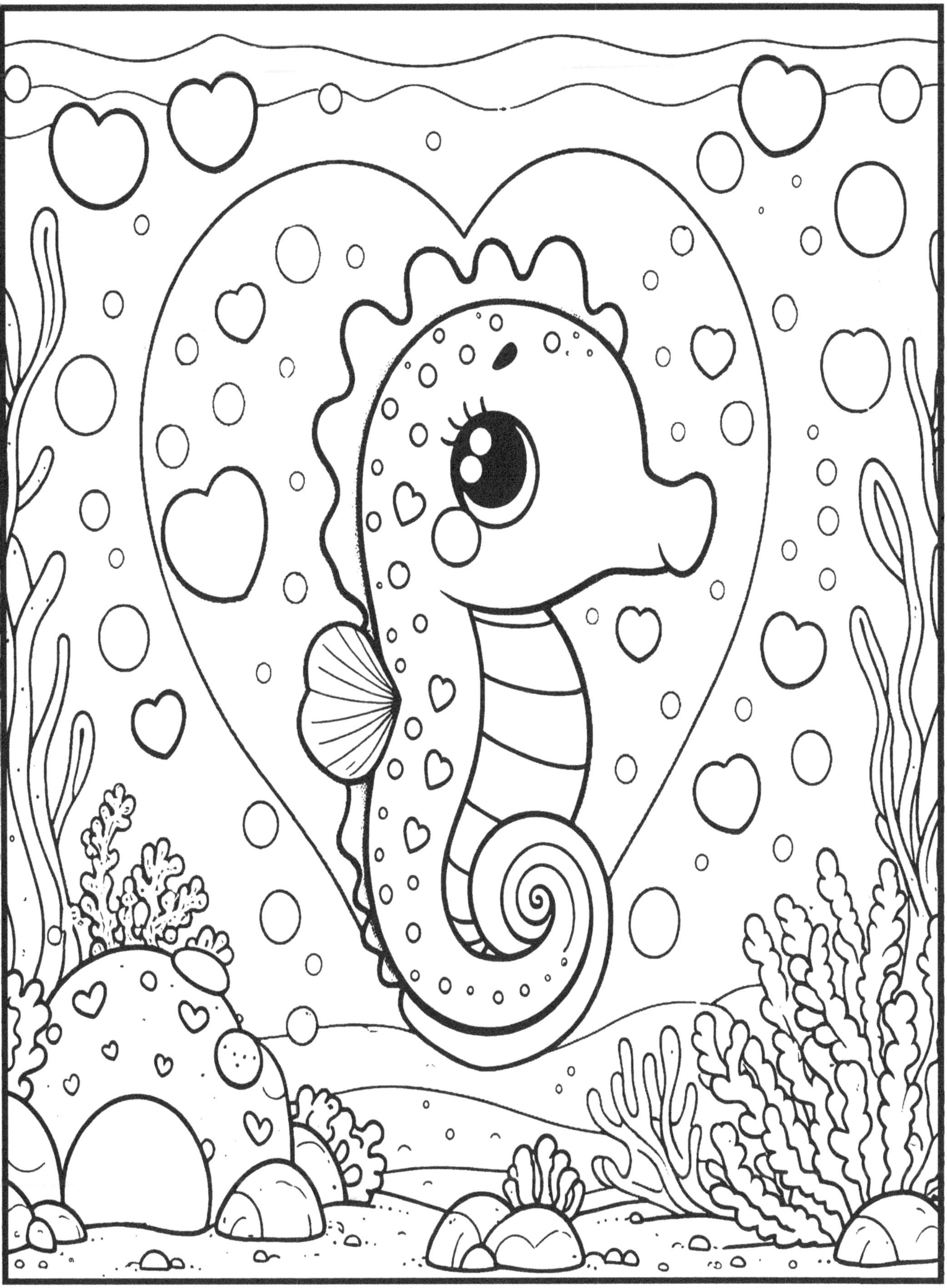

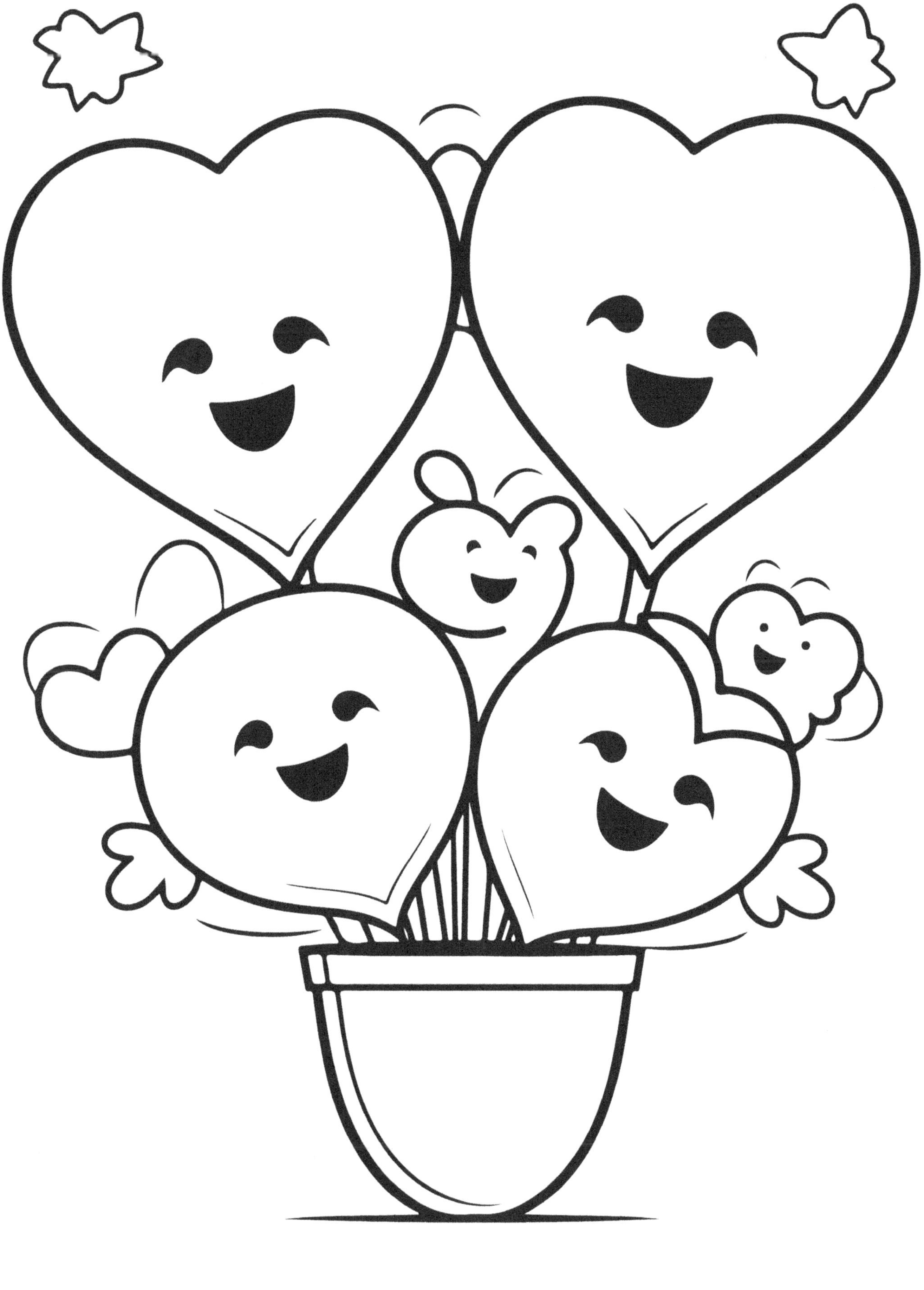

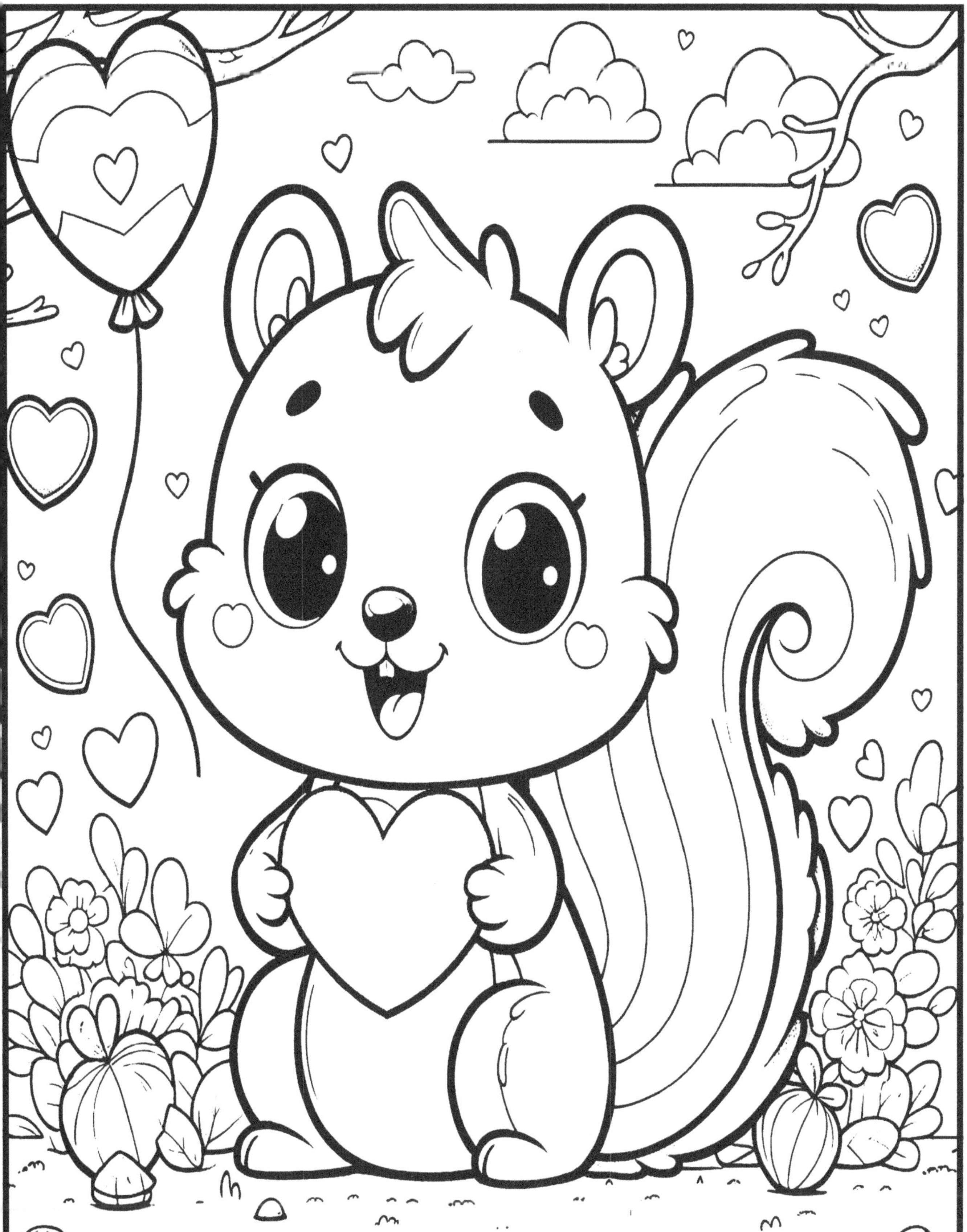

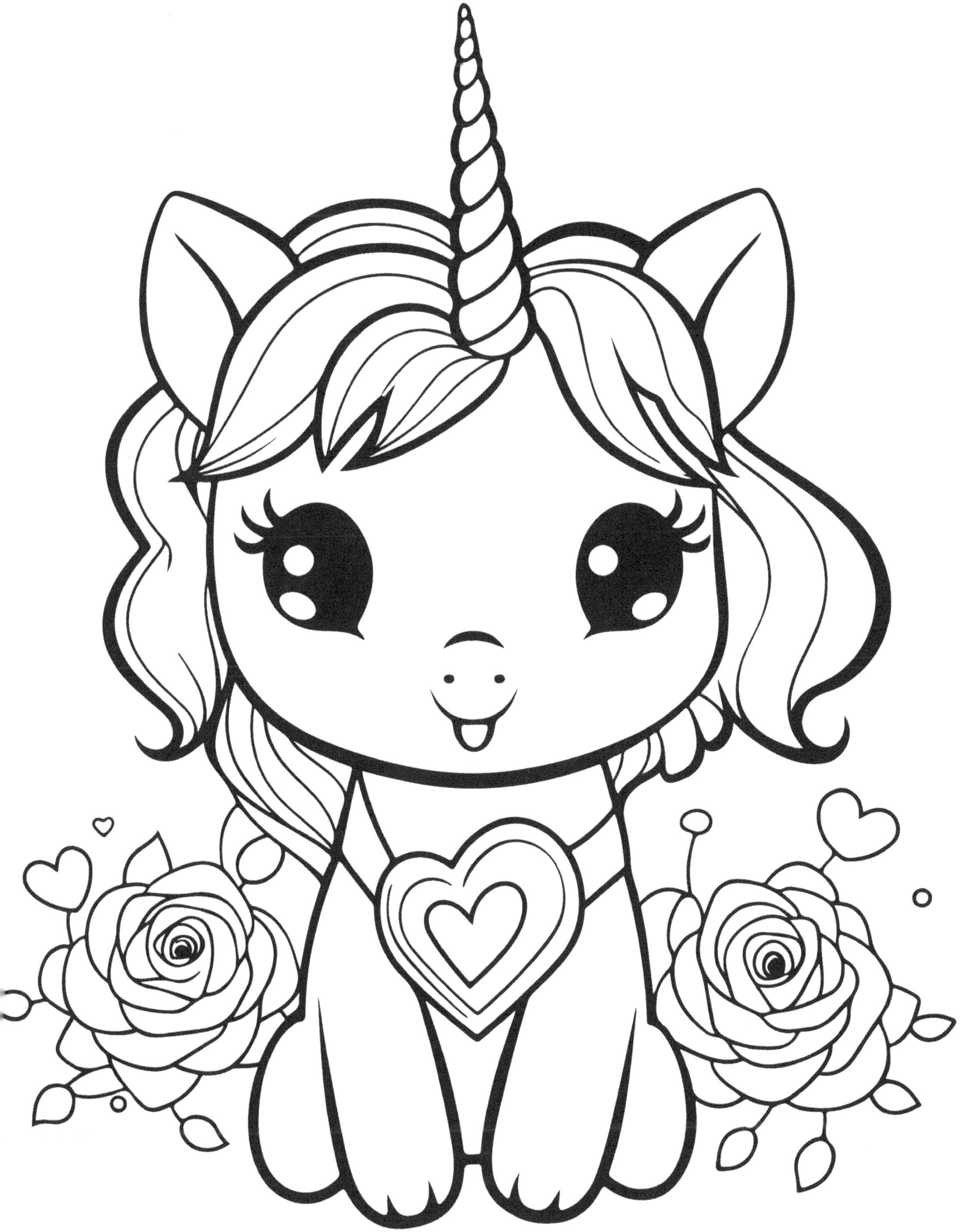

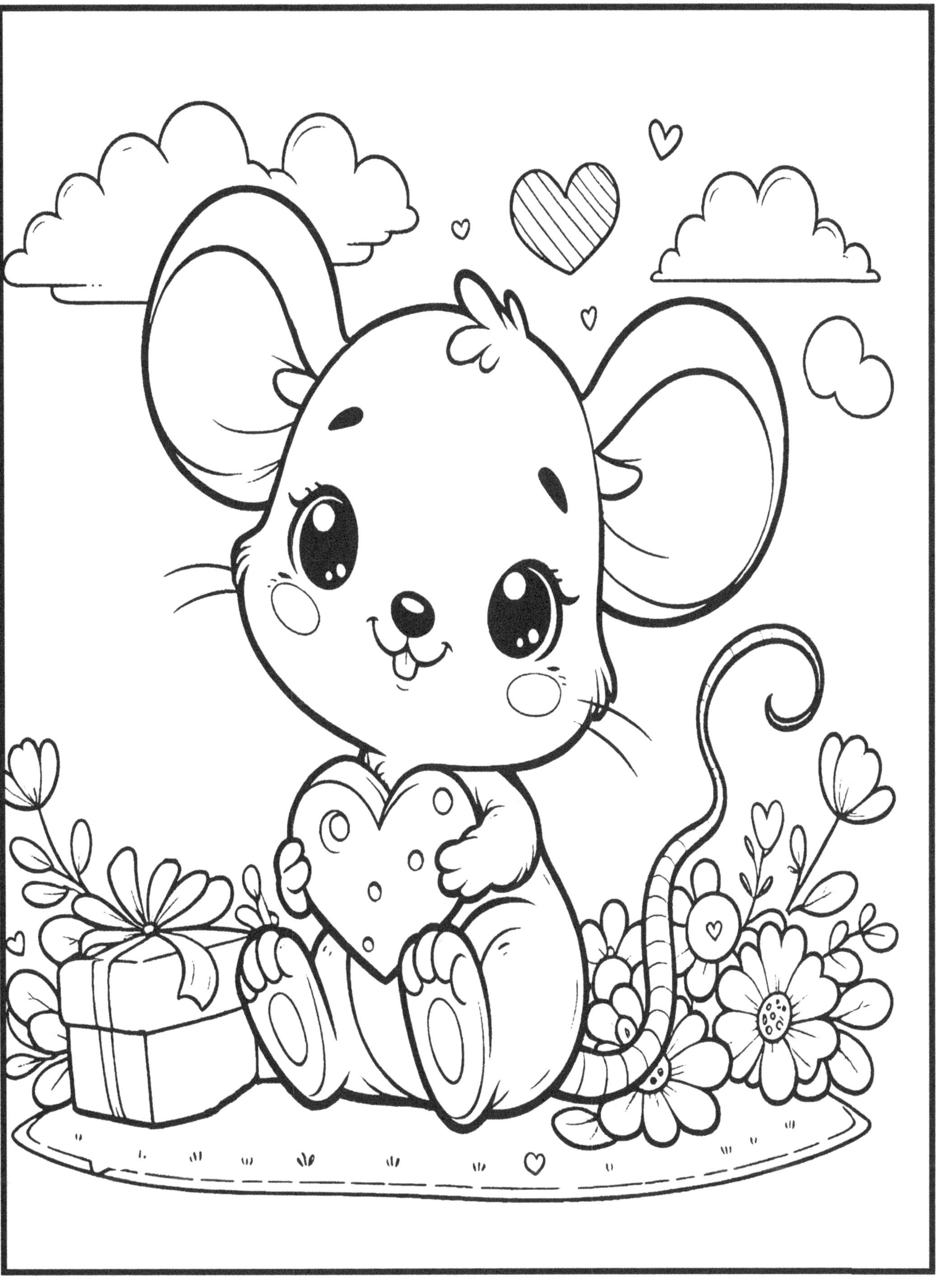

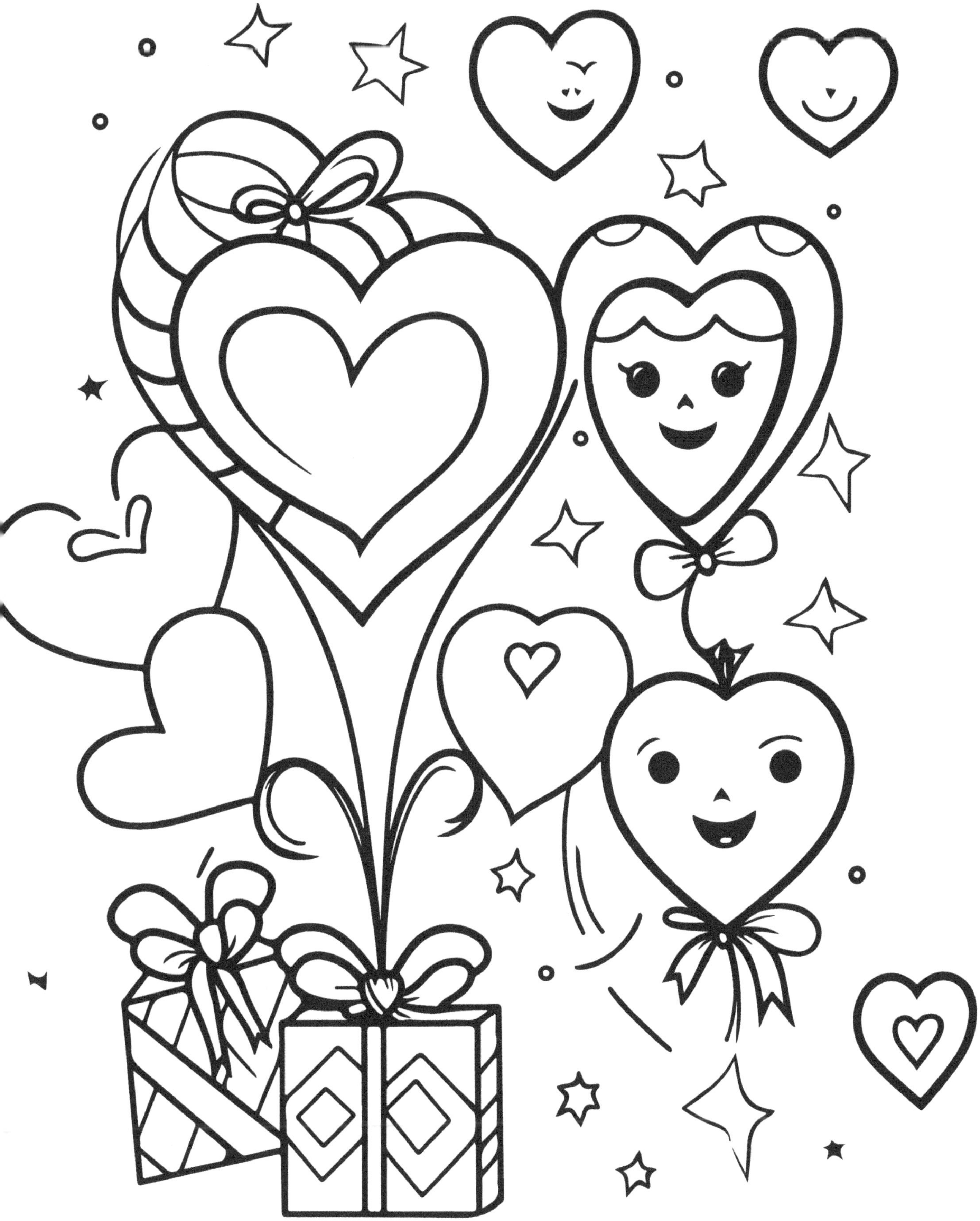

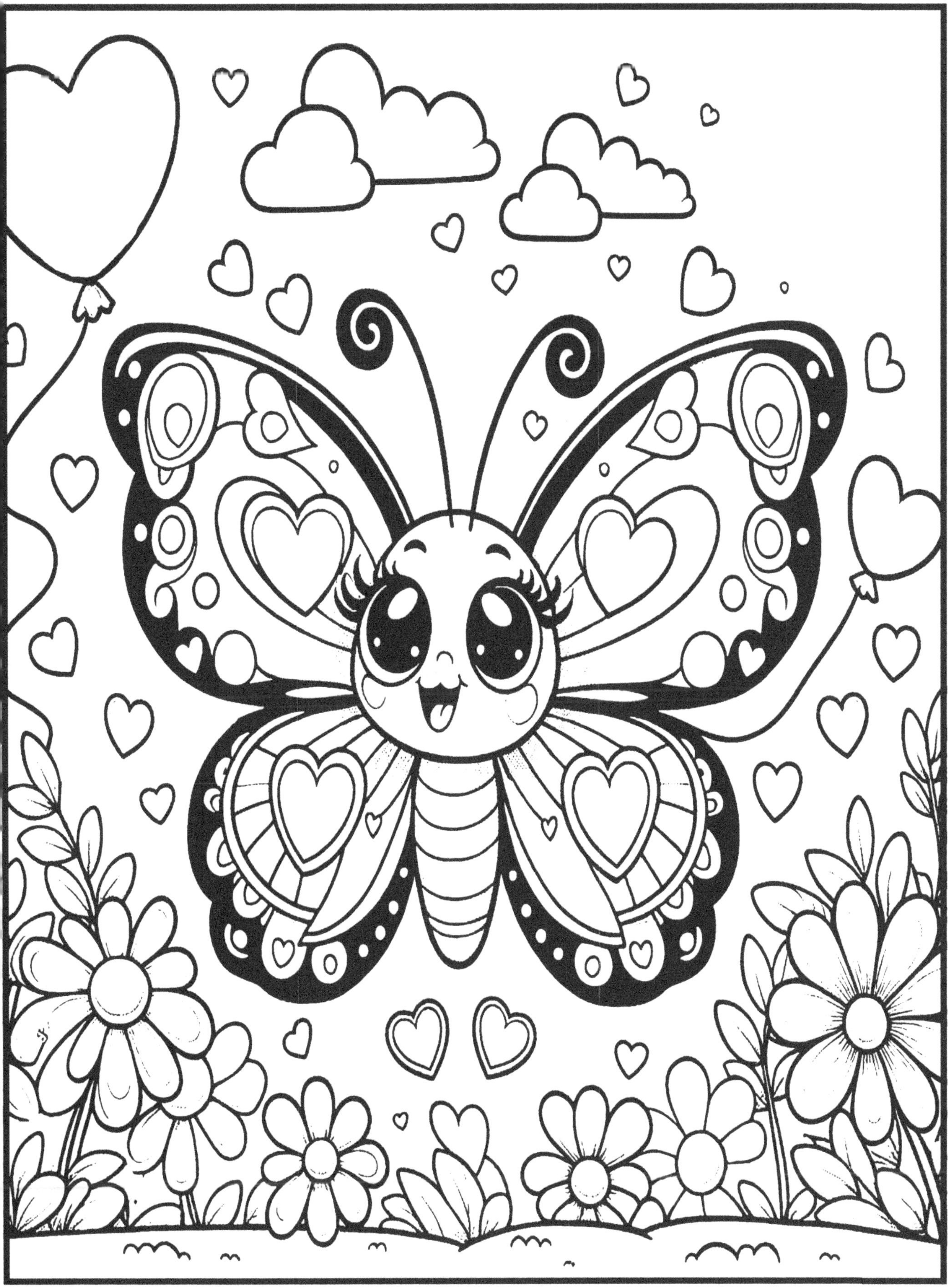

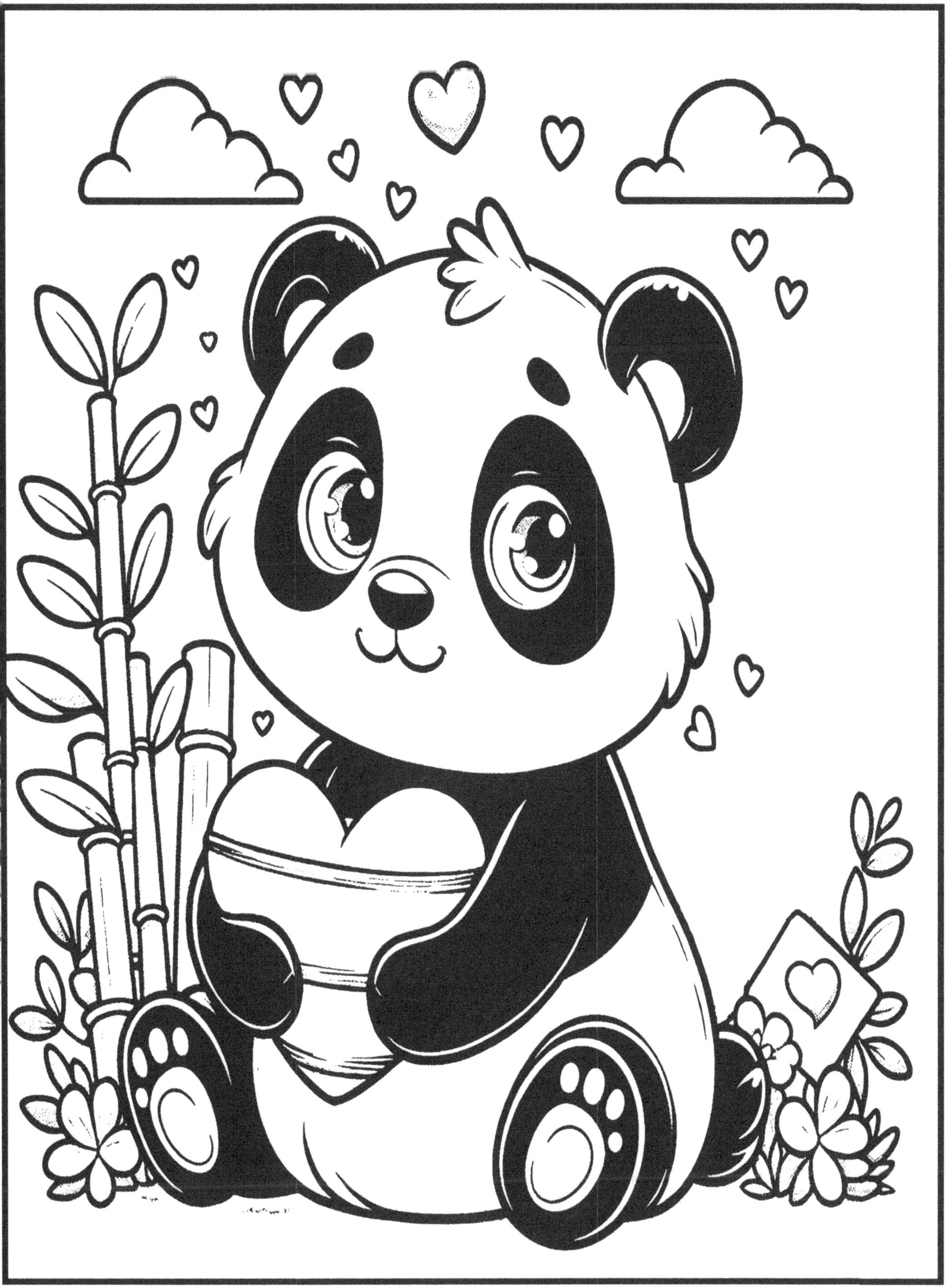

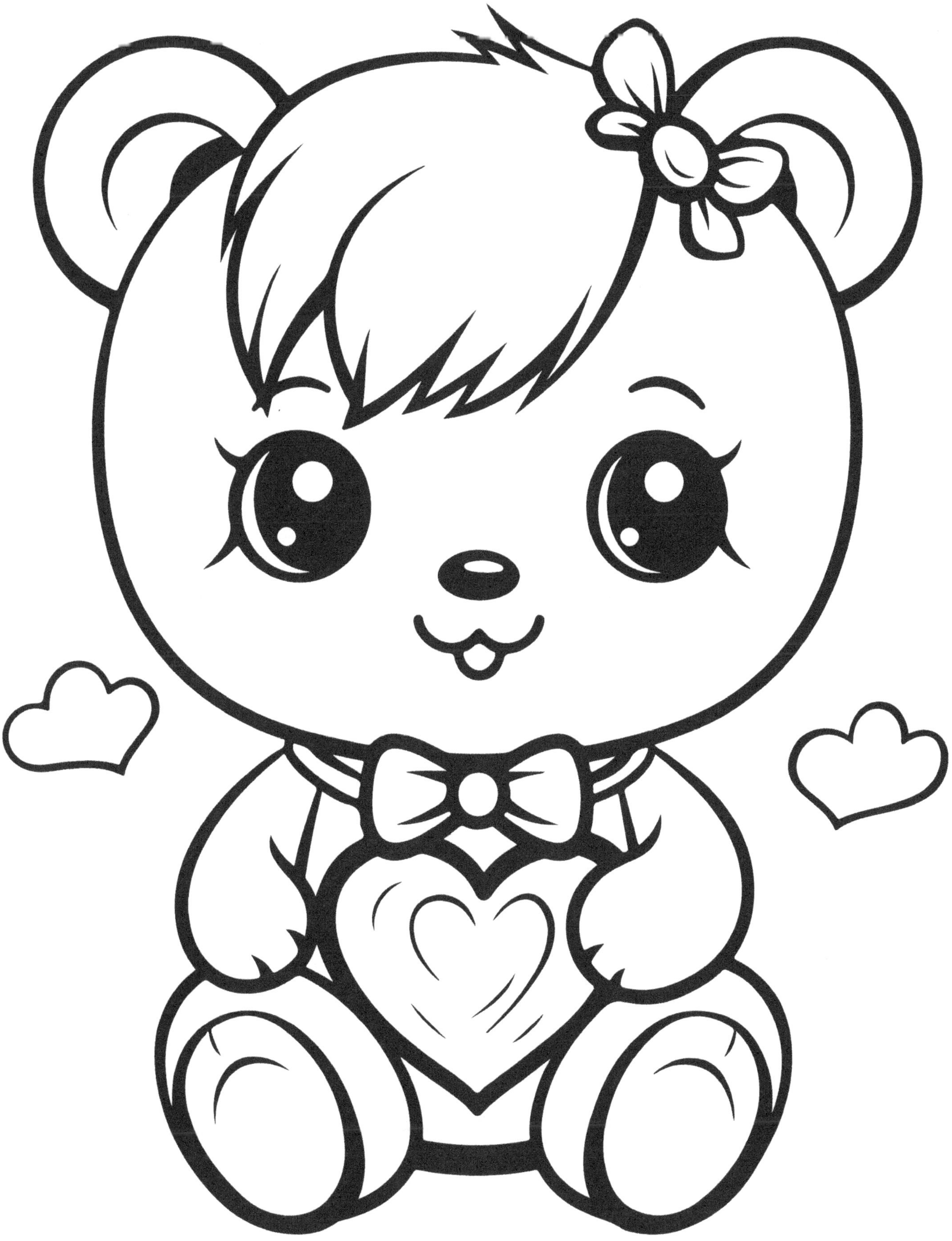

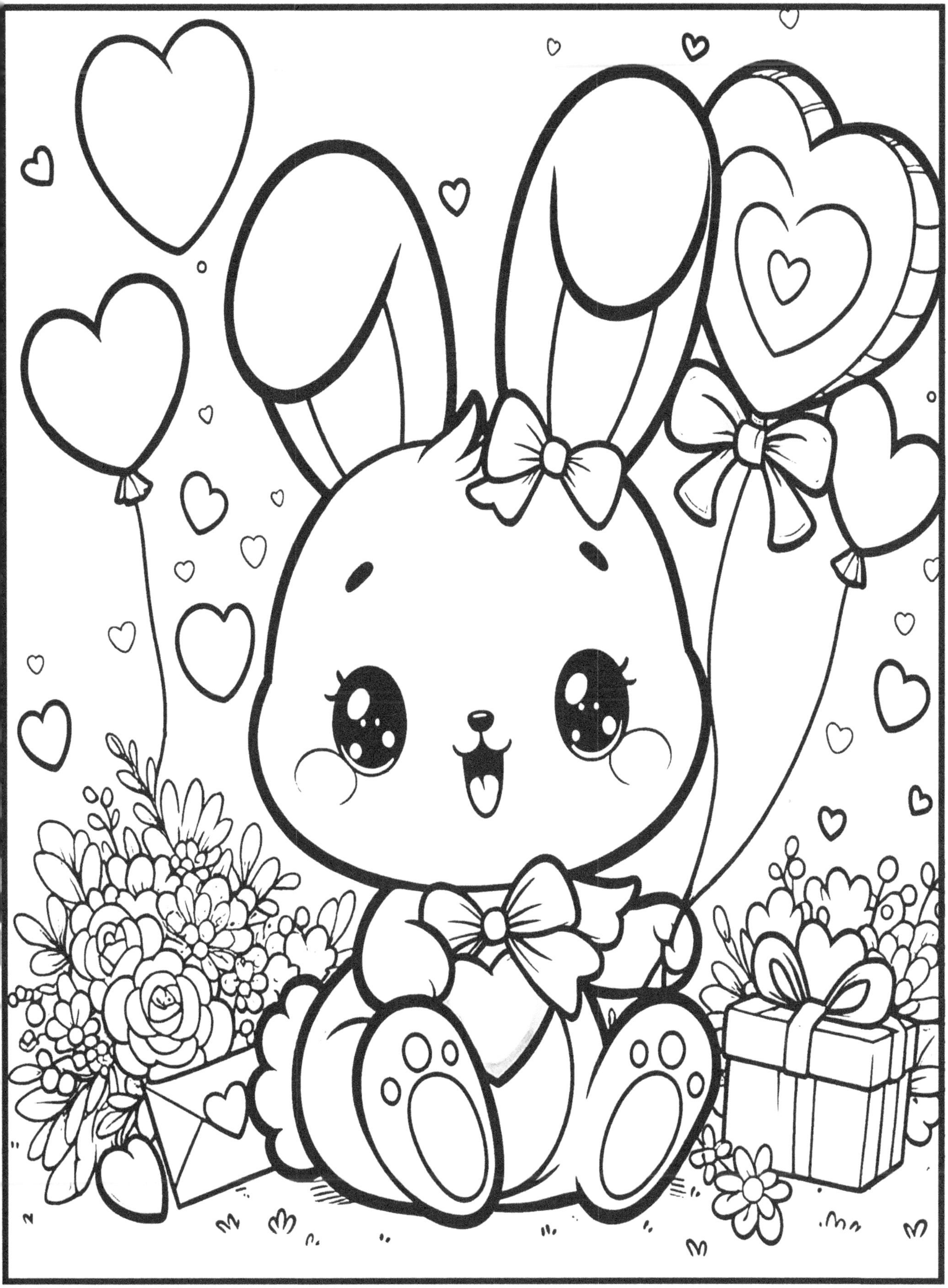

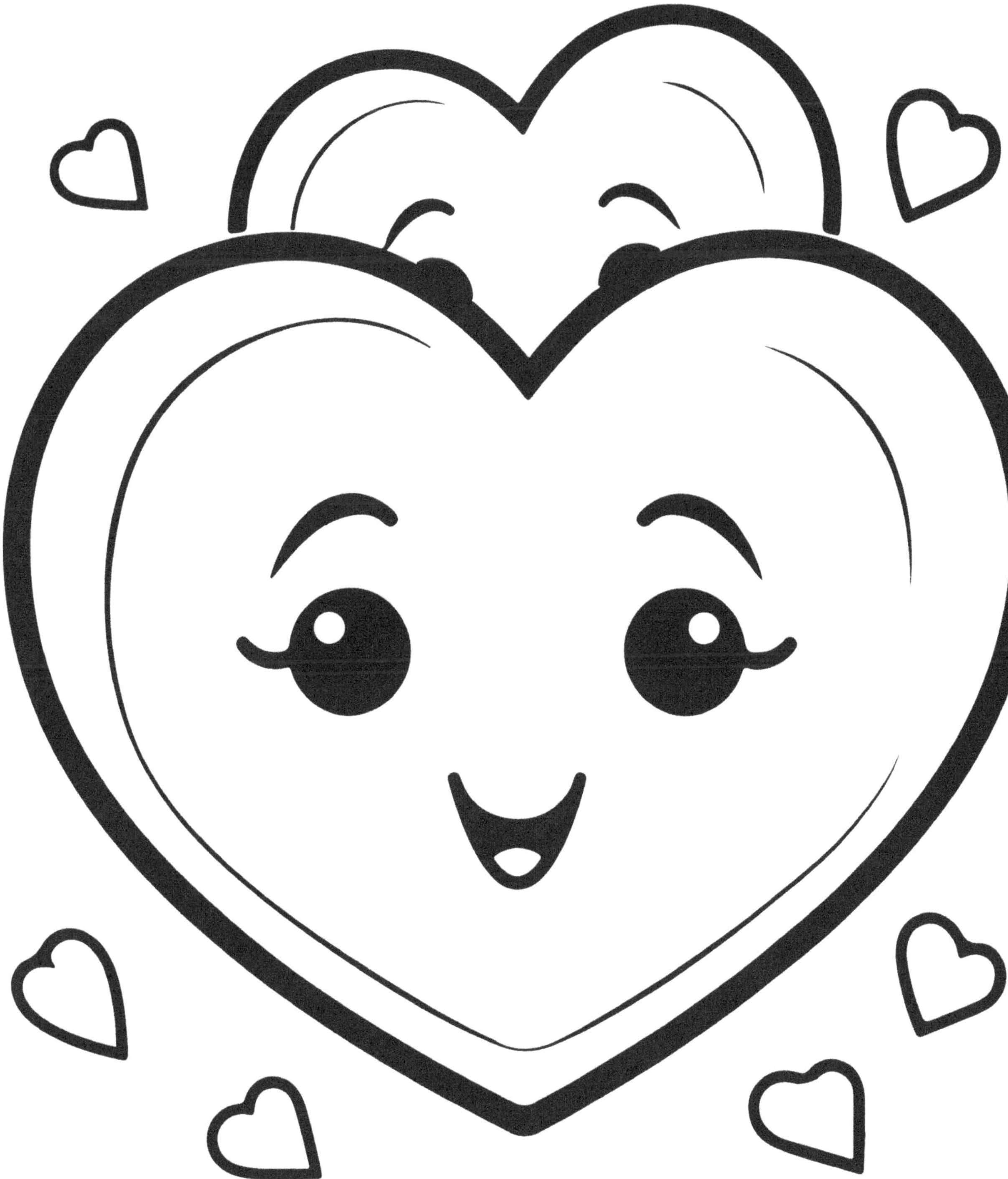

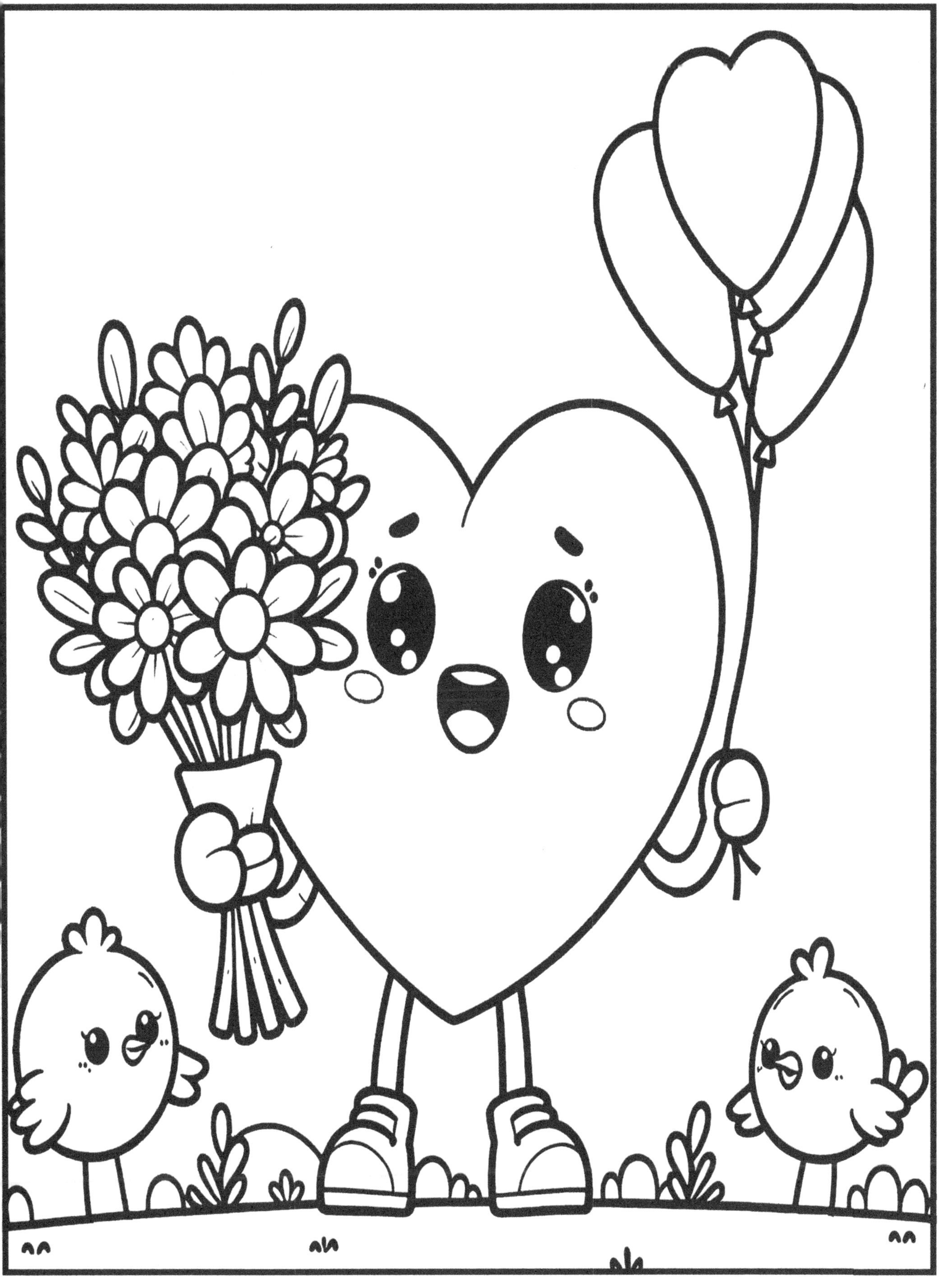

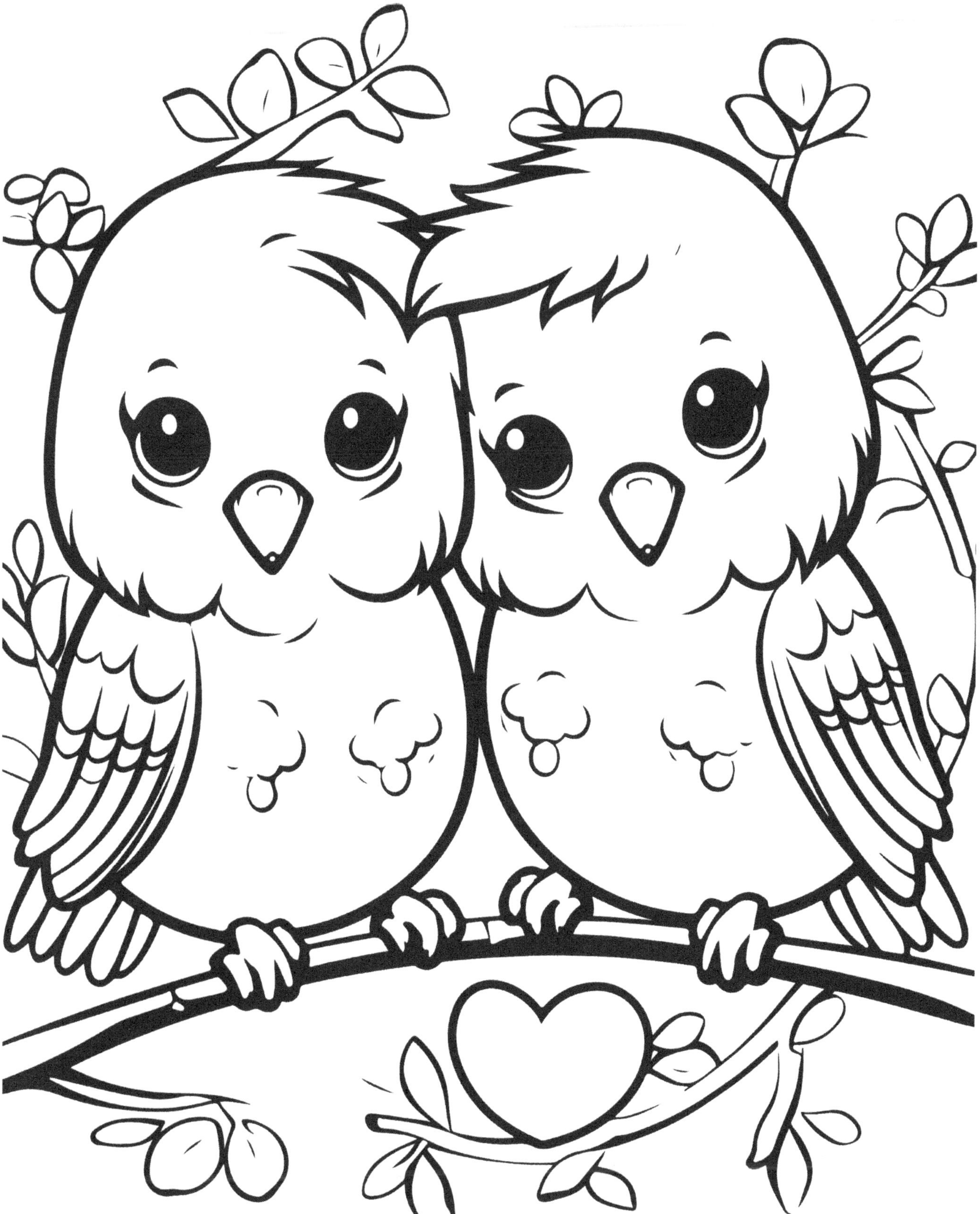

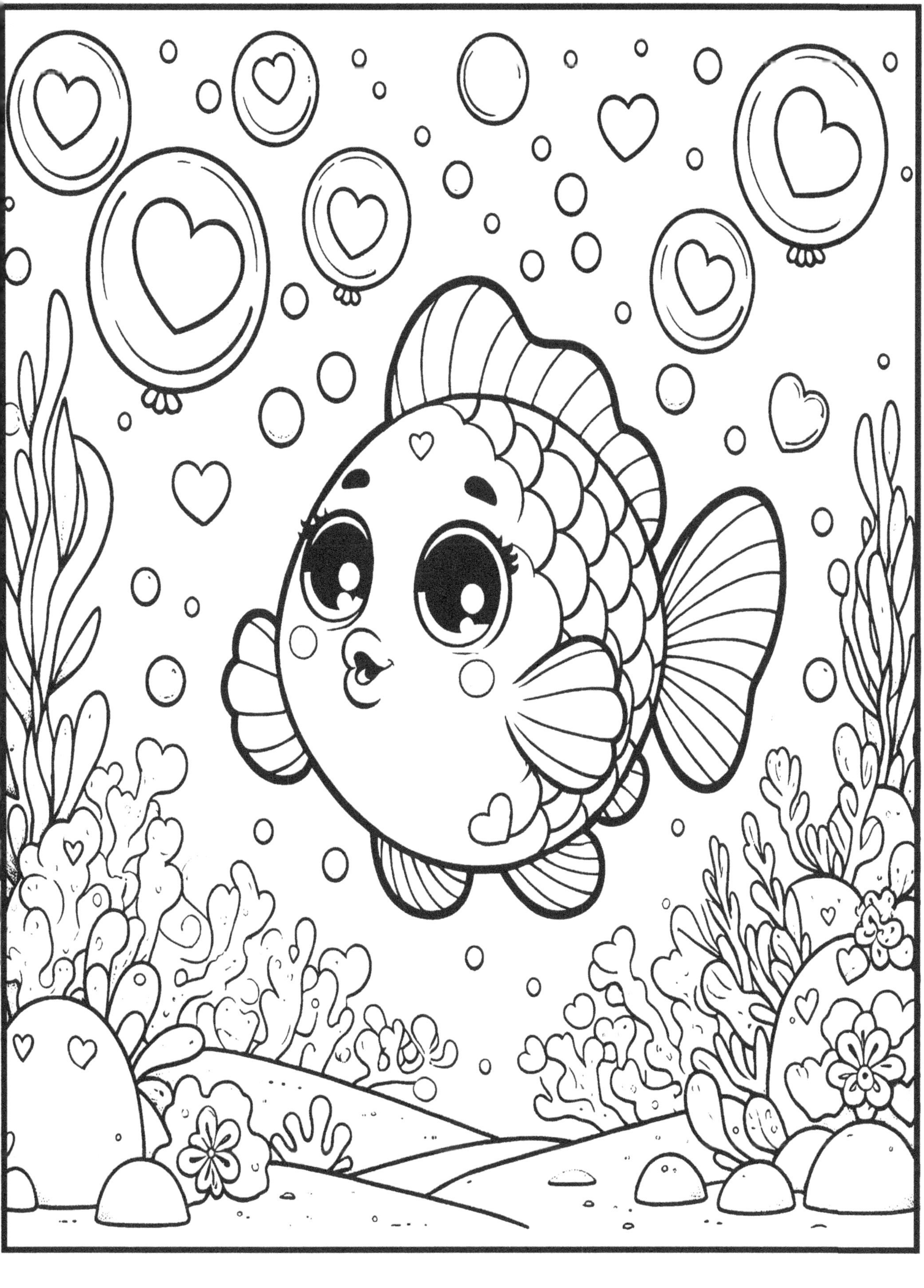

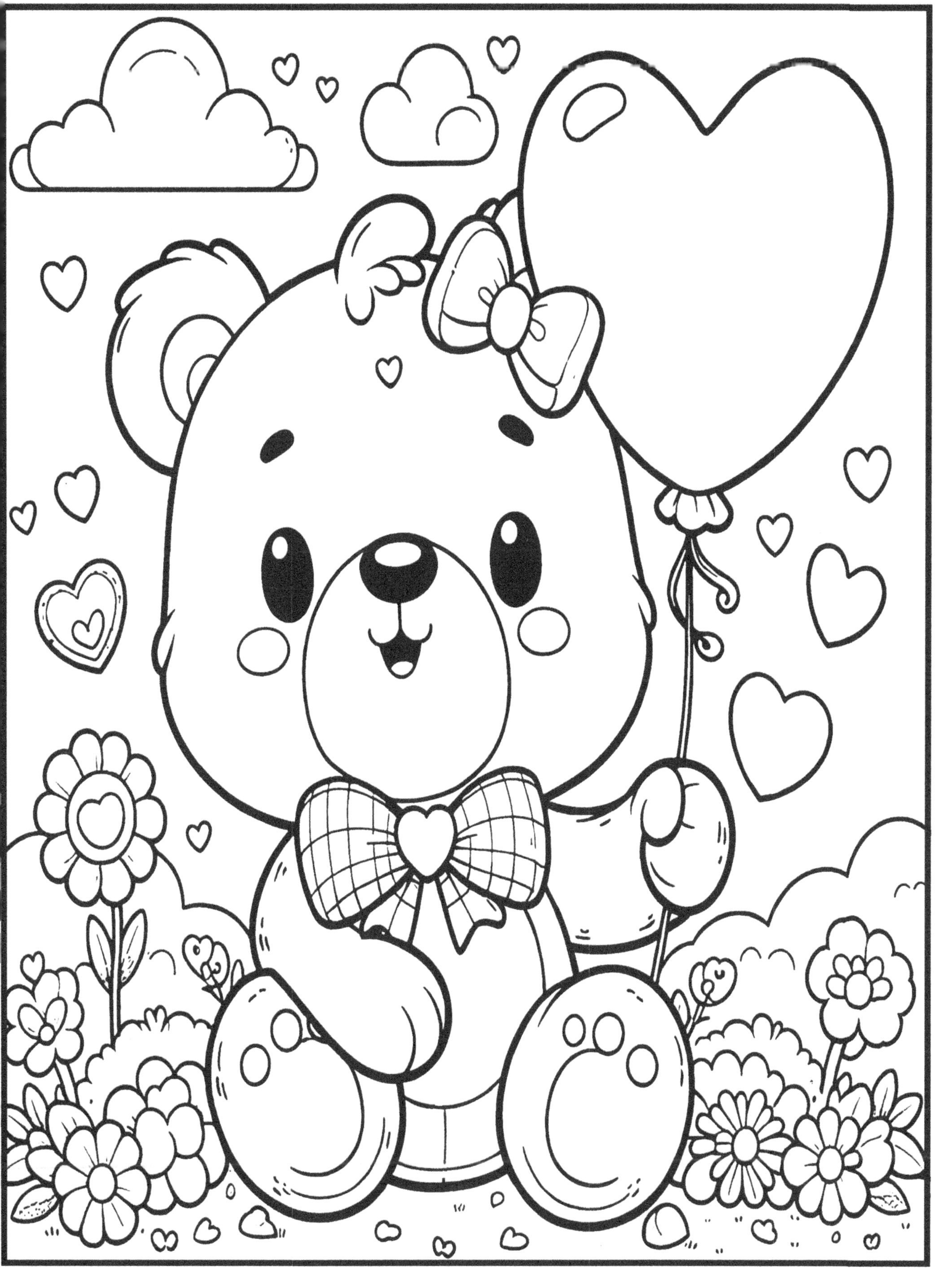

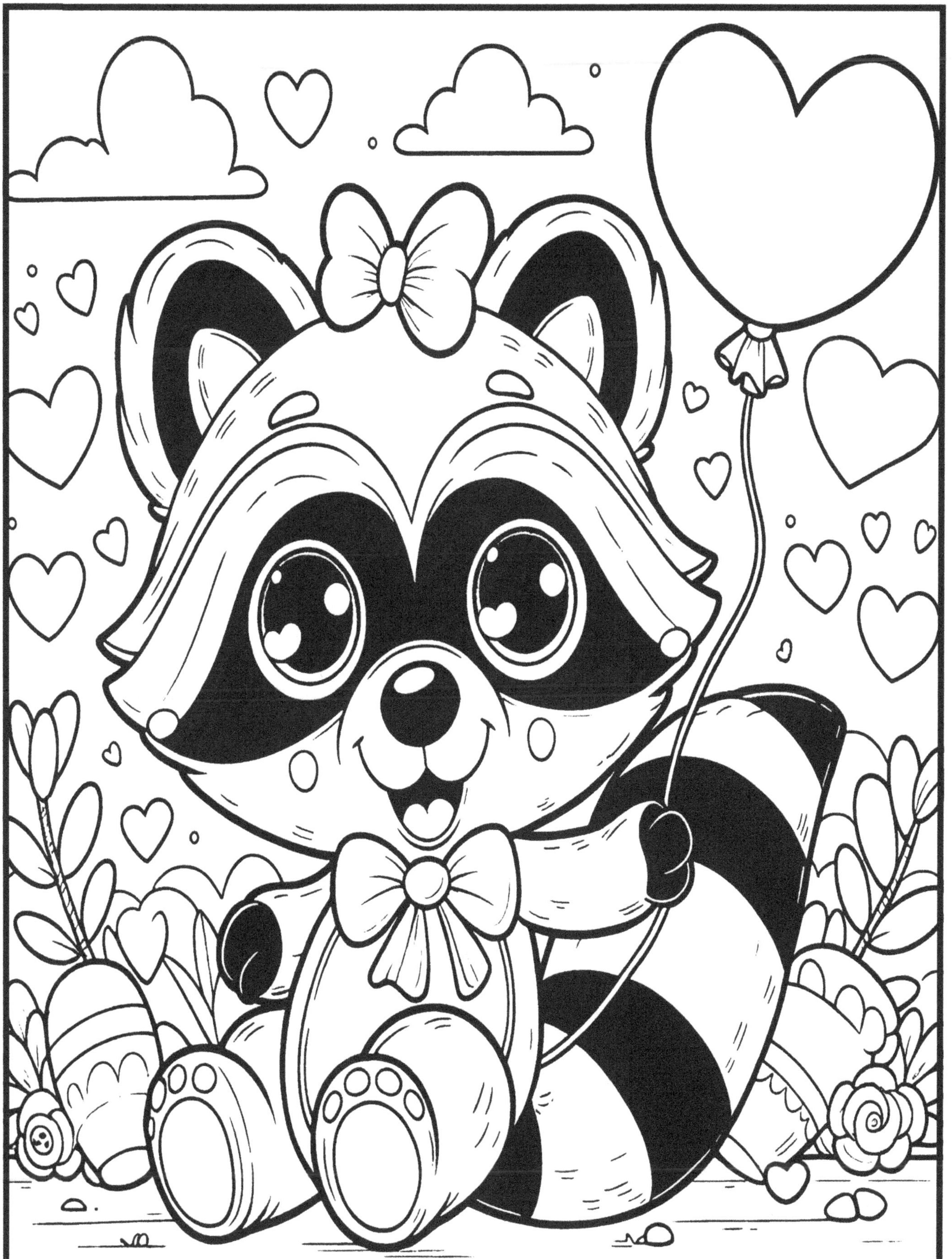

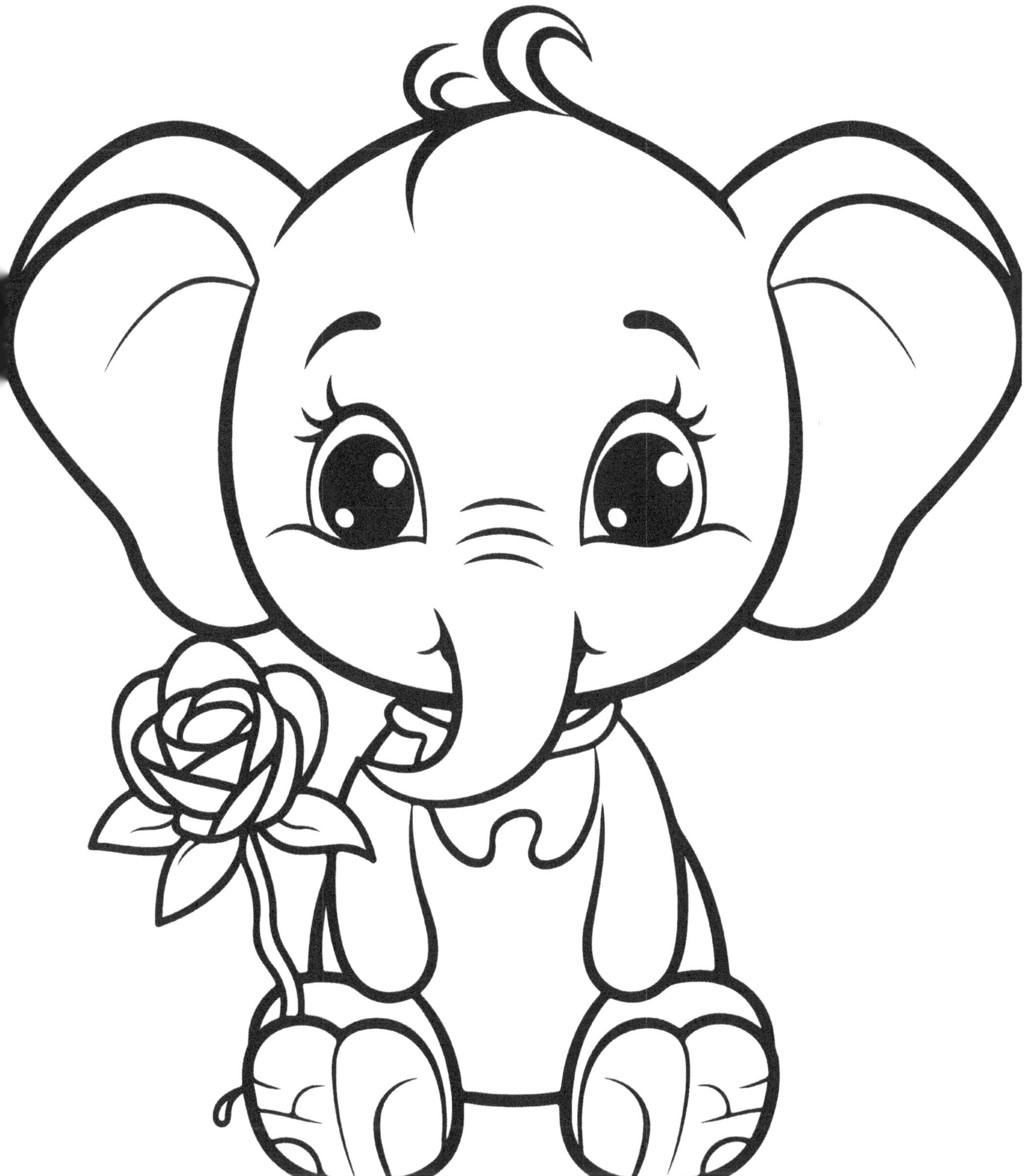

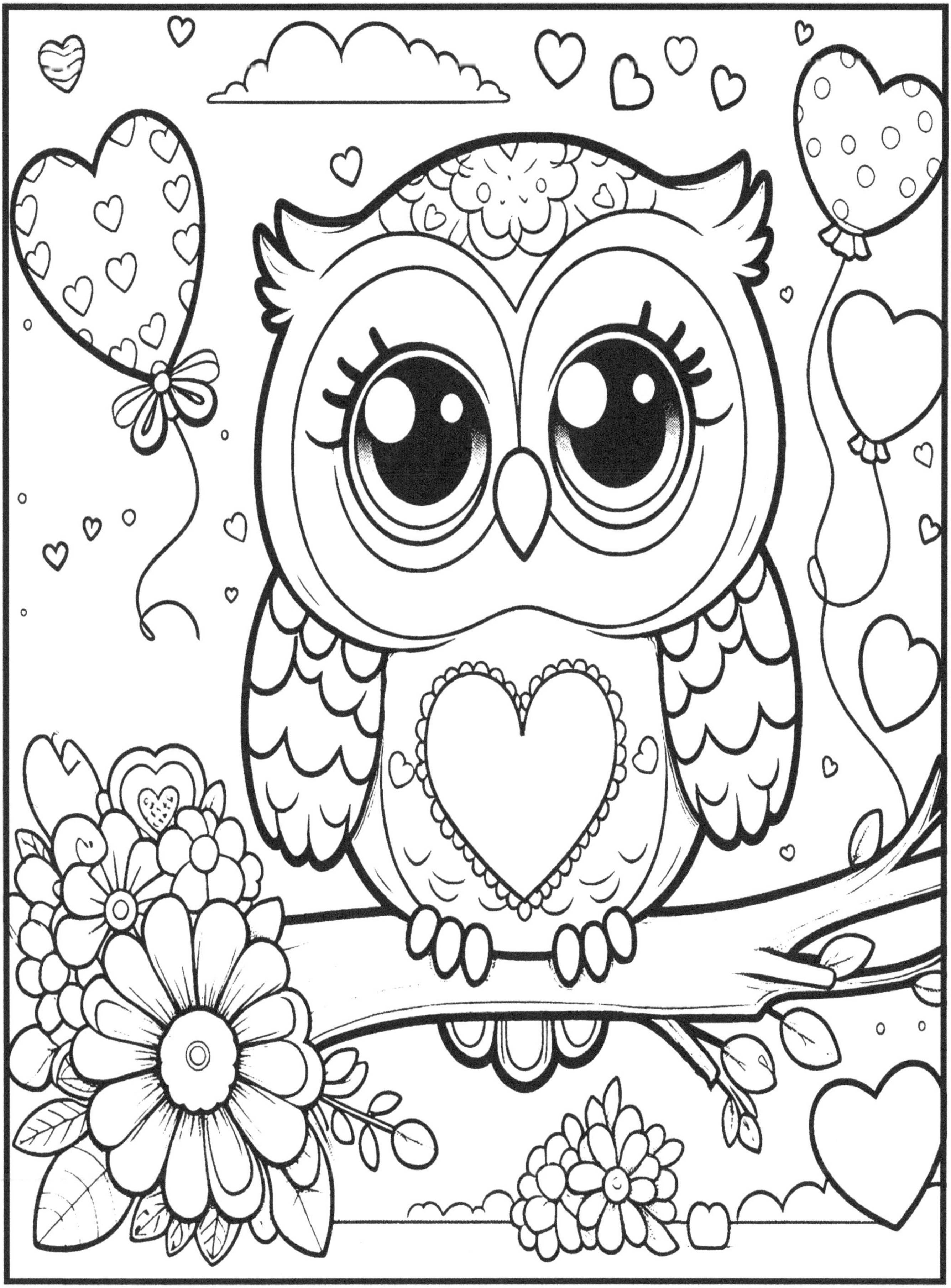

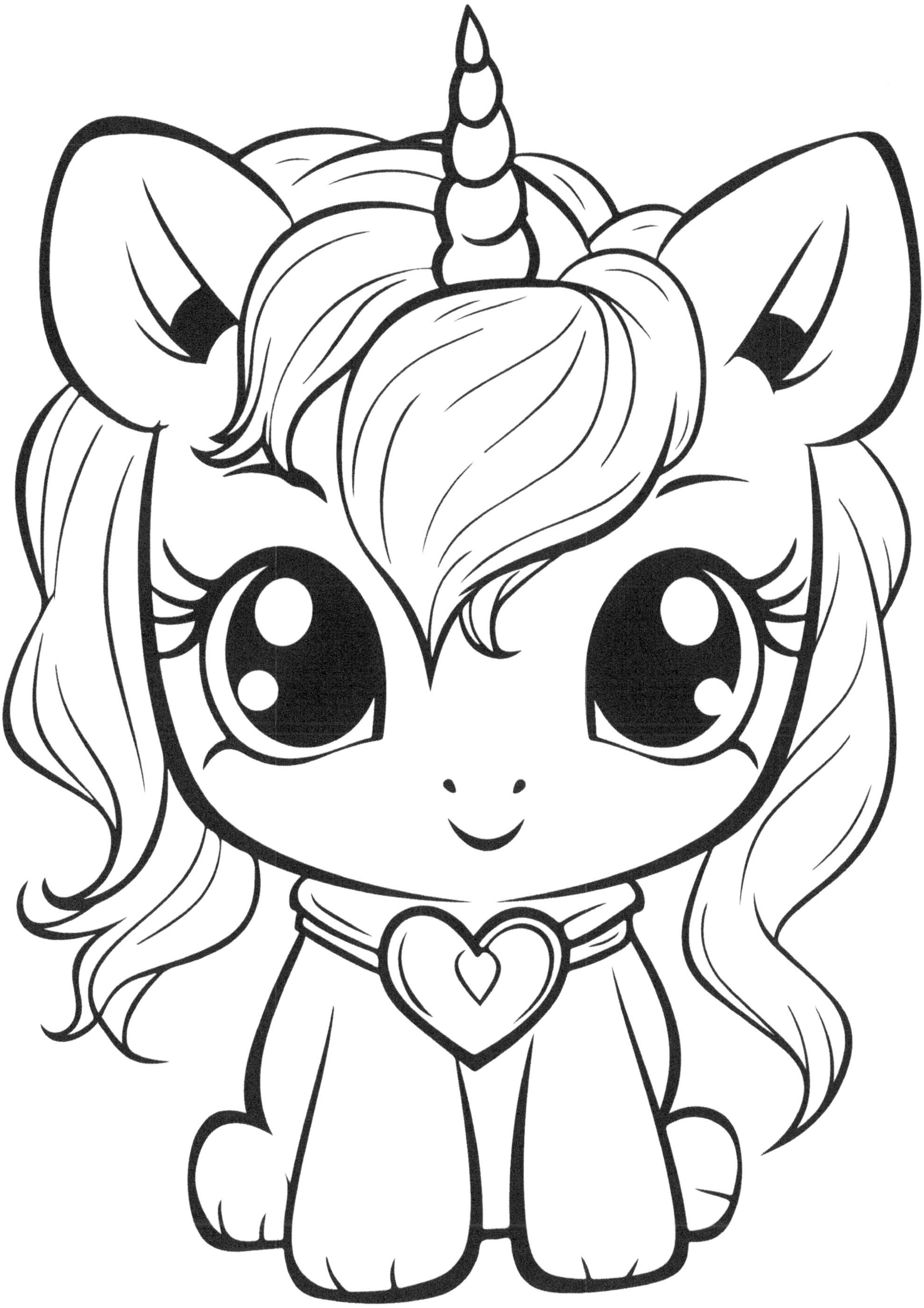

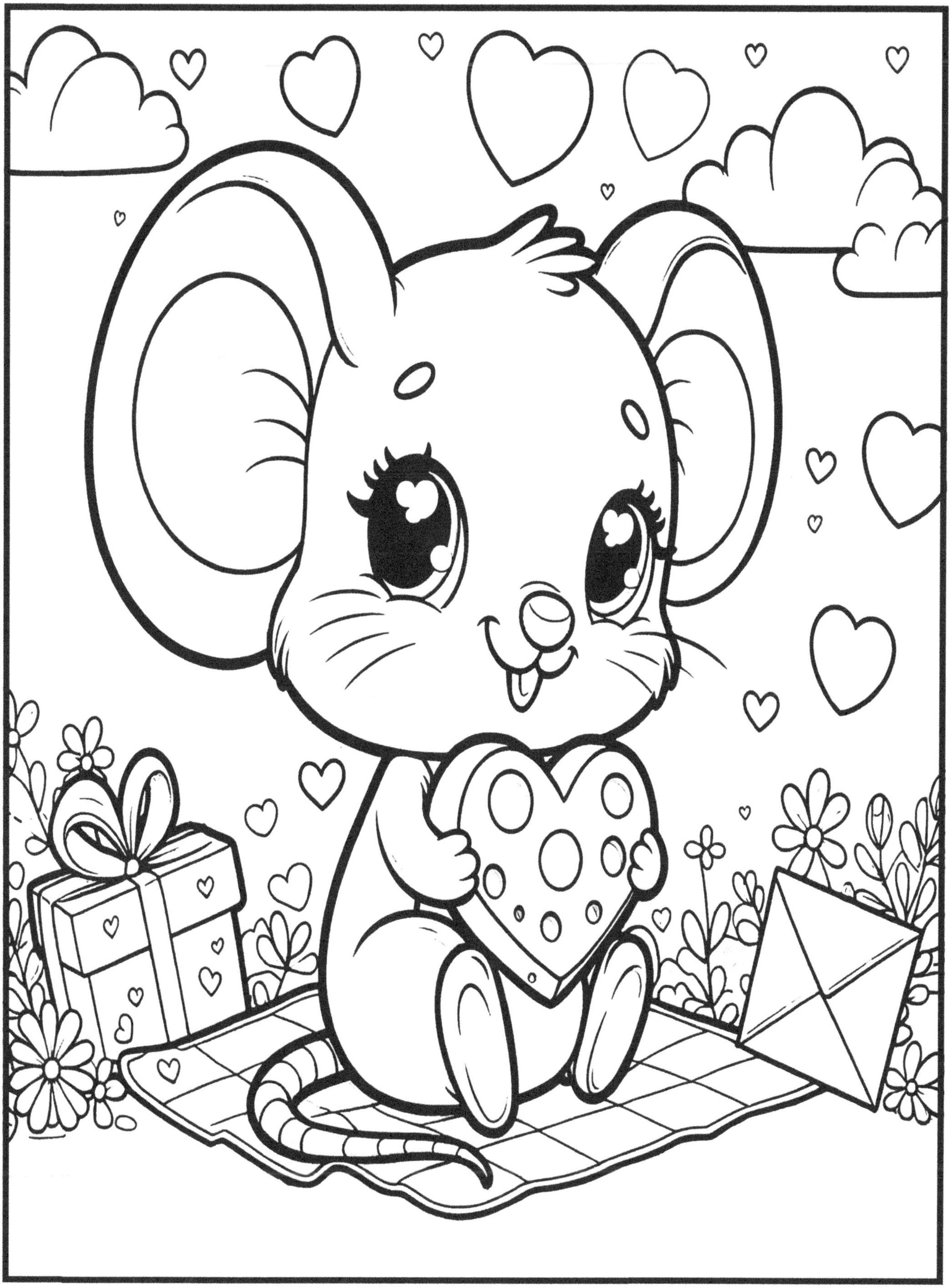

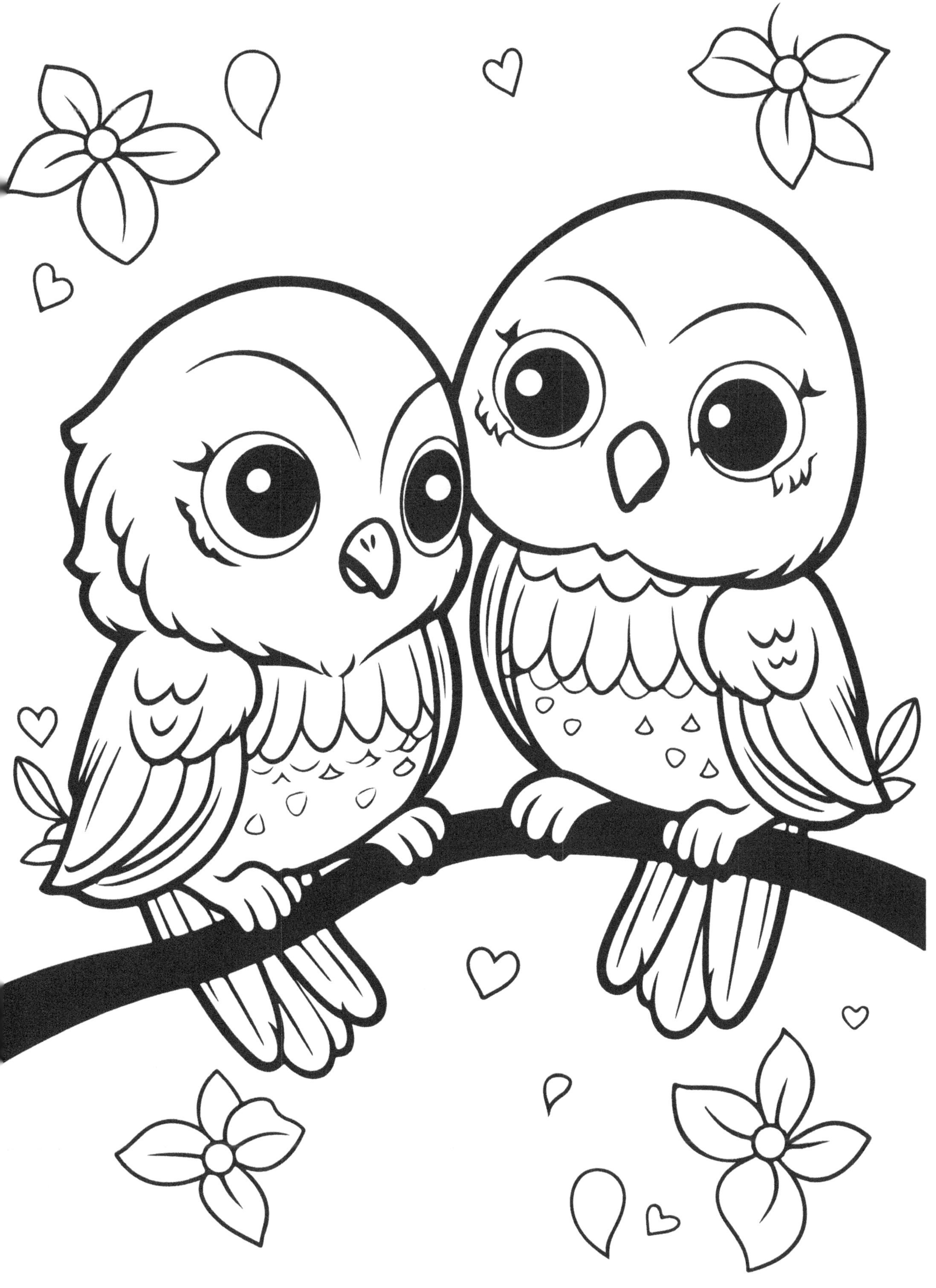

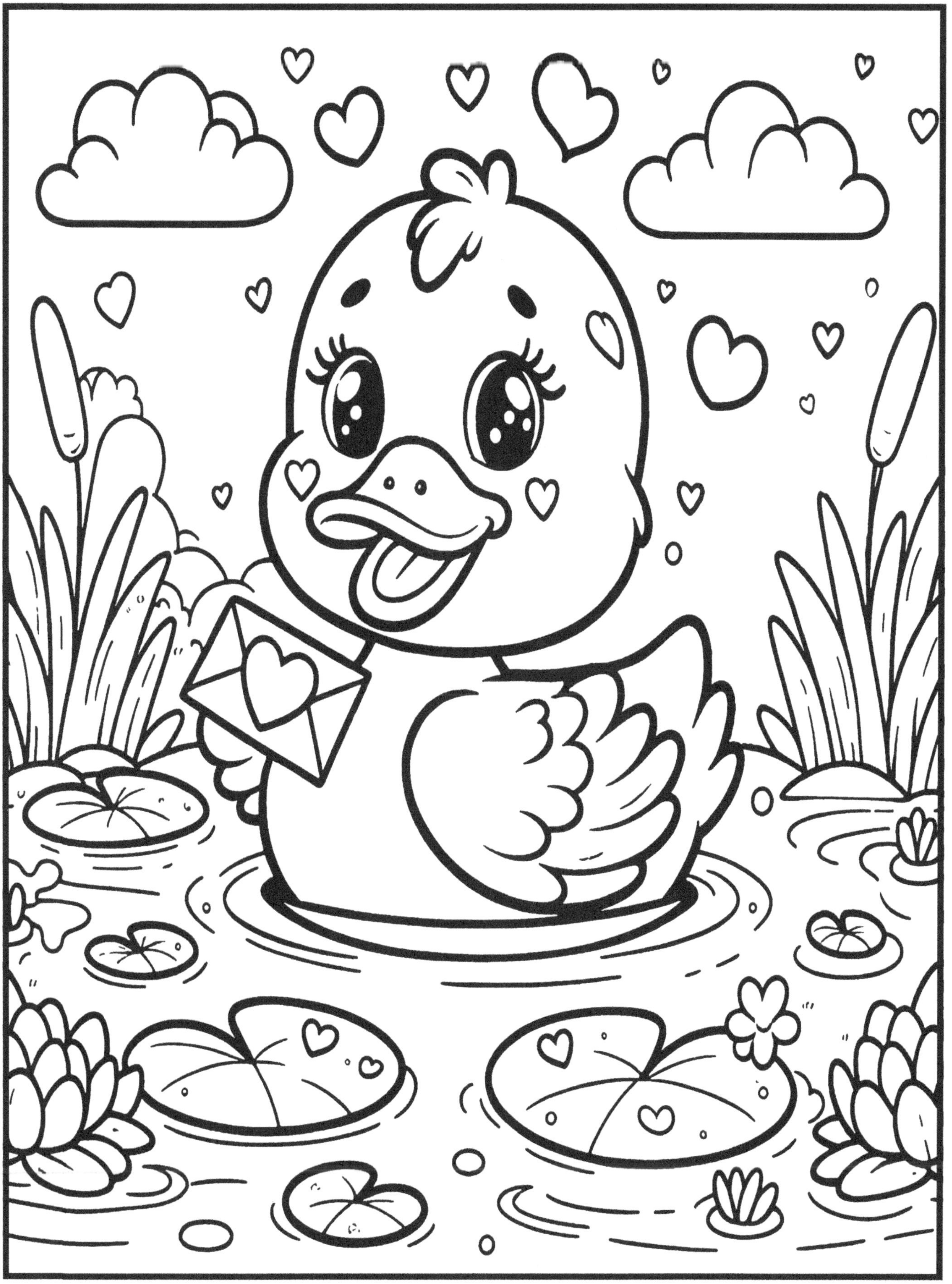

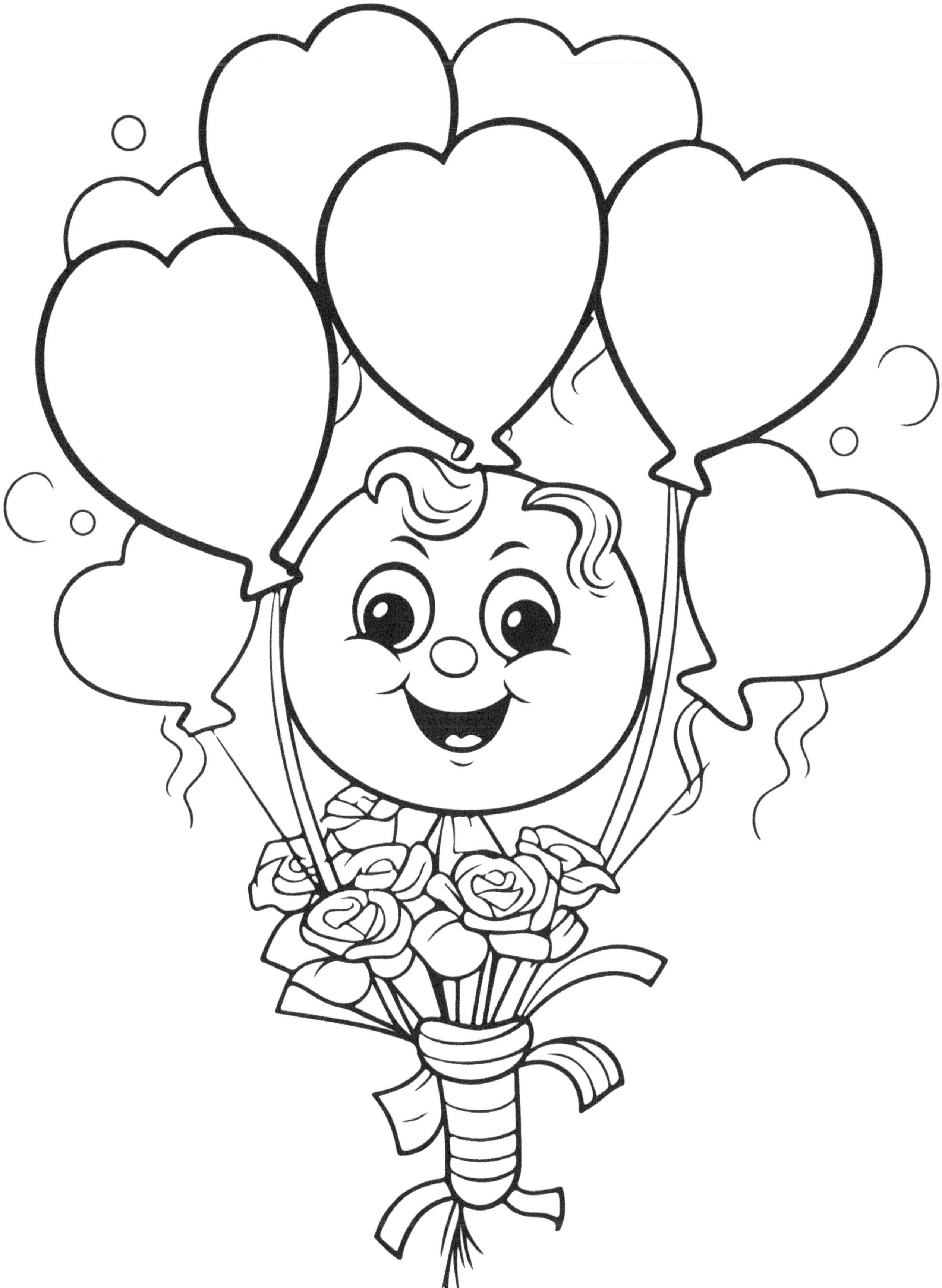

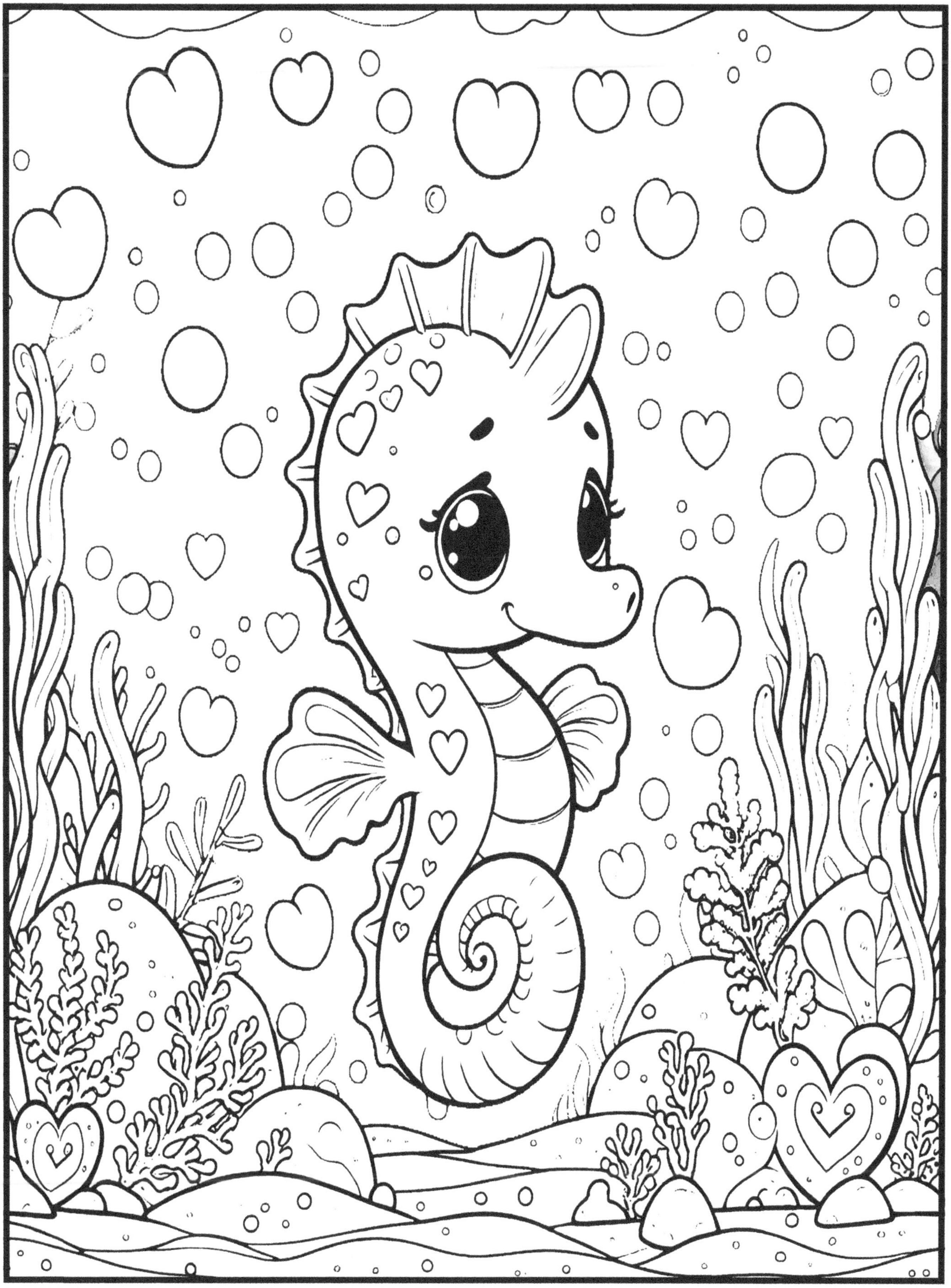

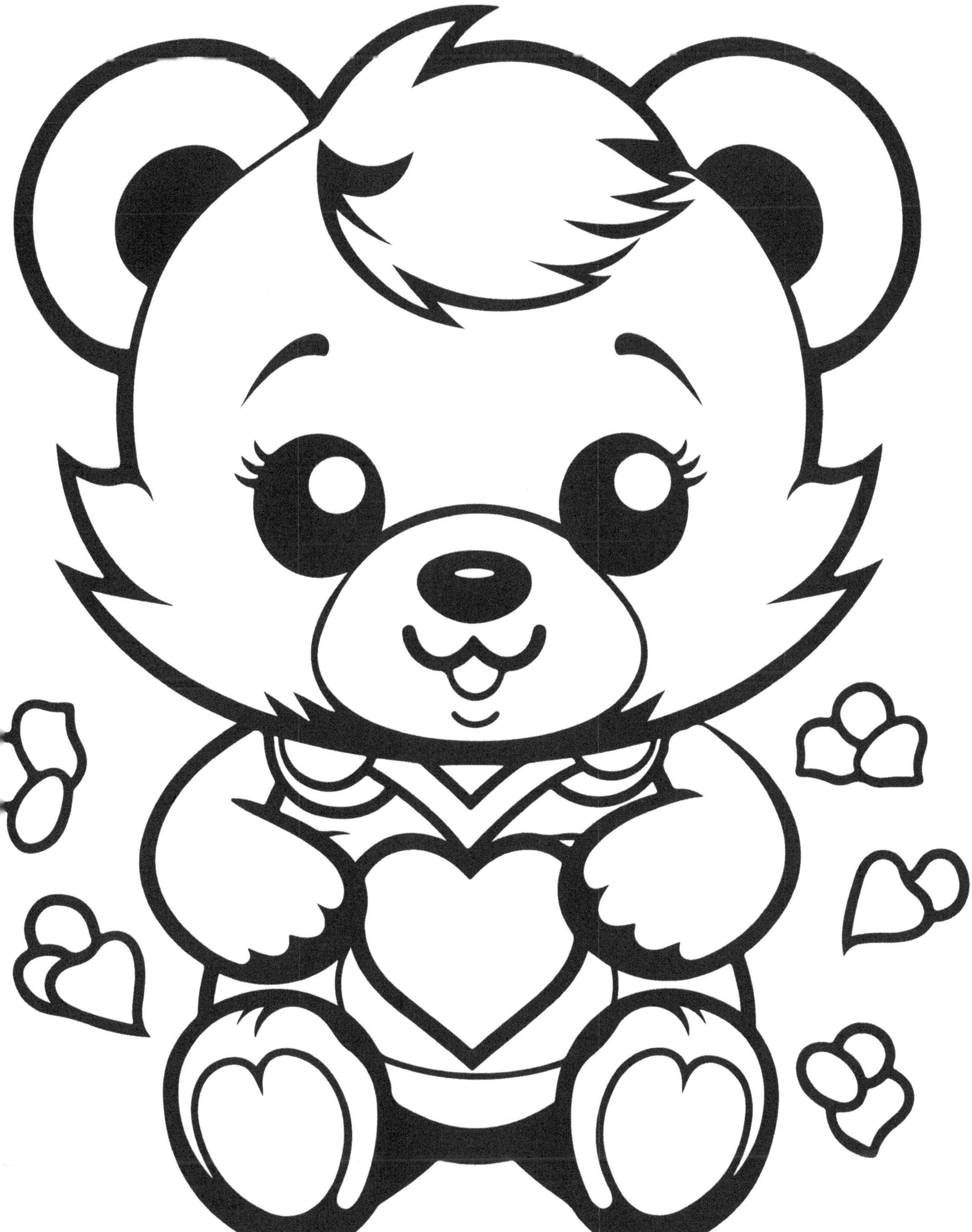

Made in the USA
Las Vegas, NV
30 January 2024

85094095R00057